My Mother and Other New Englanders

"Delivered to us in rich and vivid imagery, *My Mother and Other New Englanders* is a work of transportation. We are given passage to the family stories and history of the author, replete with faith in Christ. Their legacy of faith spills into every verse and stanza—marking even the most ordinary moments of life with renewed wonder, curiosity, and stability."

—**Josh Harp**, pastor, King of Kings Church

"*My Mother and Other New Englanders* creates a tapestry of nature and people, with the threads of faith in God as the warp and woof. As with any poetry compilation, readers will find favorites, and this reader is no exception. With the theme of New England, Erikson captures the sights and sounds of the myriad seasons while reminding the reader of the things we all hold in common as humans created in the image of God."

—**Sharon Thayer**, mother and teacher

"Having read Erikson's book of poetry, my life has been transformed—hopefully not just briefly—from a deft management of chaos to a slower and more purposeful reflection on every beautiful detail that I experience. I highly recommend this voyage through simpler times when people truly understood what it means to be patient and long-suffering, to live by faith, and to find joy in the challenge of 'making do' on very little."

—**A. L. van der Herik**, mother and author of *The Shortest Leap: The Rational Underpinnings of Faith in Jesus*

"Reading Erikson's work, I feel like an archaeologist being handed precious stones or artifacts. Some artifacts are easy to understand, while others require more pondering. One stone often has the most meaning when examined in relationship to other stones; musings, devotionals, and narratives all tied together, inviting readers to explore and celebrate family with the author."

—**Tim Sunderland**, businessman

"I really enjoyed this book of poetry. The author is a master of words, and often a tear came to my eye in reading these poems. I will definitely be reading this again."

—Eugene Van Hofwegen, retired law enforcement

My Mother and Other New Englanders

A Legacy of Faith

Susan E. Erikson

Foreword by Stephen C. Magee

RESOURCE *Publications* • Eugene, Oregon

MY MOTHER AND OTHER NEW ENGLANDERS
A Legacy of Faith

Copyright © 2022 Susan E. Erikson. All rights reserved. Except for brief quotations in critical publications or reviews, no part of this book may be reproduced in any manner without prior written permission from the publisher. Write: Permissions, Wipf and Stock Publishers, 199 W. 8th Ave., Suite 3, Eugene, OR 97401.

Resource Publications
An Imprint of Wipf and Stock Publishers
199 W. 8th Ave., Suite 3
Eugene, OR 97401

www.wipfandstock.com

PAPERBACK ISBN: 978-1-6667-5957-0
HARDCOVER ISBN: 978-1-6667-5958-7
EBOOK ISBN: 978-1-6667-5959-4

12/19/22

Seaway Boats, Rosborough Boats USA, used by permission. www.easternboats.com.

Scripture quotations are from the ESV® Bible (The Holy Bible, English Standard Version®), copyright© 2001 by Crossway Bibles, a publishing ministry of Good News Publishers. Used by permission. All rights reserved.

Dedication

This book is dedicated to the memory of John and Nettie. They have been gone for over 30 years. I still have a few of the letters they wrote me when I was a girl. When I read them, I can hear their voices and see them just the way they were. It comes rushing back.

Their generation spanned the great chasm between the horse and buggy era and a man on the moon. It was a period of huge upheaval—two American presidents assassinated; two world wars; the Great Depression; massive cultural and technological changes—all within their lifetime. They kept a firm hold on those things that mattered most and made practical decisions as they straddled both worlds. The wood stove at the camp stayed, but an updated kitchen made more sense. Keep the outhouse, add indoor plumbing. At the Concord house, in the 1940s, they renovated the upstairs bathroom and kitchen, but the pull chain toilet stayed. When they moved downstairs in the 1960s, after Nancy died, the downstairs bathroom and kitchen were ushered into the 20th century. No more grand copper tub. But the rest of the house looked the same as it had been since the end of the nineteenth century. The wallpaper I remember looked like it had been original to the house's antebellum construction.

I miss them and look forward to renewing conversations in heaven. It will be good to see them again.

Contents

Foreword | ix
Introduction | xi

Spring

Spring | 3
Pilgrim Heart | 4
Pilgrims | 6
Going to Meeting | 9
Sorting | 11
Ice-Out | 12
John's Ice-Out Recipe 1973–1983 | 13
Muddying | 15
Sugar Maples in March | 17
Behold the Rain | 18
Spider Hike | 20
New Baby 1929 | 21
She Is an Artist | 23
She Loves to Read | 24
She Is an Independent Woman | 26
Her Name Is Music | 28
Sugar Hill in June | 31
Petal Snow | 33

Summer

Summer Is | 37
Summer | 38
Skunk Trouble 1915 | 40
Temptation | 43
John's Boats | 45
Blueberry Picking with Nancy | 49
Traveling | 51
Dockside | 55
Stone on Stone | 56
Memories | 59
Life with John | 61
Fishing Therapy | 63
Milkman | 65
Boat Errands 1960s | 68
John's Fireworks 1940s | 71
John's Garden | 73
Timber Blues | 76
Summer Life | 78

Autumn

Autumn | 81
Changing Weather | 82

First Blush | 84
Change | 86
Huskin' Party 1896–1902 | 87
Good Cider | 89
Cranberry Time at the Old
    Stone House | 91
Leftovers | 93
Good Flavors | 95
Leaf Peeping Along
    the Kanc | 98
Autumn Breeze | 100
On Hurricanes | 102
We Never Waste a
    Thing | 104
Connections | 107
Sanctifying Grace | 109
The Walk | 112
Last Fall | 114
Prayer for
    Consummation | 116

Winter

First Snow | 121
Ghost Trees | 122
Winter Joy | 124
Two Friends | 126
In January | 128
XC Skiing | 130
Skinning | 132

The End of Talks | 134
The Girl Beneath | 135
My Mother's House | 138
Pilgrim Faith | 141
In Step | 143
More | 145
Until He Comes | 147
Now, Not Yet | 149
Grace | 150
Waiting | 152
A Time to Heal | 154
Their Last Battle | 156
Mount Hope Cemetery,
    Loudon | 158
He Is My Rock | 160
Hope | 162

Remembering

Remembering | 165
The Old Stone House | 167
Hiram 1807–1892 | 170
Nancy 1868–1961 | 173
John 1893–1988 | 179
By Faith: Nettie
    1895–1986 | 182
Waiting in the Shadows:
    Sylvia 1929– | 185
Nelson 1938– | 188
Gathered In | 191

Foreword

Susan Erikson's delightful volume of poetry regarding faith and nature in the New England setting is organized by season, with a closing section entitled "Remembering." Written in the great Puritan tradition of John Flavel's *Navigation Spiritualized*, Susan uses the recollections of past generations, and her own personal experiences over the years to draw us back to our New England roots and beyond those beginnings to a heavenly home. Hers is a pilgrim work, and she invites her readers along for that fruitful journey. In her writing one cannot help but hear the echoes of favorite passages from the Bible and snippets of historic hymns alongside the commonplace of New England life. A pastor could easily imagine using verses from the author's poetry to help the hearts of his congregation to consider better their days here in New Hampshire soil and to gaze beyond our current moments to that land where we will soon behold a more permanent place to thrive.

Susan's portrait of her mother (and others) is very inspiring for all of us. Her writing is an offering of tender love and admiration. One cannot help but think of the command, "Honor your father and your mother, that your days may be long in the land that the Lord your God is giving you."

Those with some personal history in the Northeast will find that the author has lent her words to describe experiences that we have faced in our own lives. As just one example, many young ones will relate to a poem like "Temptation" where the poet describes the first swim of the season. The boldest thrill seekers are soon racing back to shore for a towel to provide some relief from the very chilly waters.

FOREWORD

The author gives us realism both in her natural and spiritual observations. Poems like "Sanctifying Grace" tells us of the struggling man who only reaches Journey's End through death. Particularly at the end of the volume, Susan excels in communicating the complexity of future loss anticipated as time takes its toll. Yet she grieves as one who has hope. Those in Christ will surely "know the joys of greater days."

This is a book that should be read over and over again. We have more to learn from it as we ourselves age. What a great gift to give to others both young and old! May many see the beauty of a hard life well lived, marked in the character development of those who have already finished their races here below. May others, through the lovingly crafted words of the author, catch a first glimpse of the One who through His life and death has secured for us the best of all possible resurrection homes.

Pastor Stephen C. Magee
Exeter Presbyterian Church, New Hampshire

Introduction

My mother was born the year the stock market crashed. It was fortuitous that she entered this world into one of the many areas most prepared for the Depression—the "make do" and "do without" centers of the universe. Even words were used sparingly, its inhabitants not wanting to waste a thing. This book is about her and the people I came from—at least some from the New England contingency. This is her world, and the world of her ancestors. And as her daughter, it is my world as well.

While unpacking my family history, I uncovered a bold genetic path that runs from the mass migration of Puritans and other dissenters that settled in places all along the New England coast, to the people I knew and loved: ancestors fiercely committed to God, to family, to hard work, frugal living, and independent thinking. Being surrounded by taciturn, hard-working, independent, thrifty sorts tends to create curmudgeons; but it also builds a strong sense of place, a certainty about life, and a never-give-up attitude. These Puritan impulses are imprinted across my own DNA, and I often feel more at home among the white birch, and the lakes and granite cliffs carved by massive glaciers.

The family stories that are the backdrop for the poems of this book come from a number of sources. In the 1960s, my father recorded personal interviews of both my mother's parents that I have since transcribed. While my grandmother Nettie contributed a few personal interviews, the bulk of the recordings are my grandfather John's experiences and memories. In 1996, my mother and a distant cousin put together a detailed history of the Cate family based on recollections, documents, and photographs. My mother,

INTRODUCTION

her youngest brother, and his wife, have all provided valuable information based on their own recollections of growing up. And of course, I have my own memories. My grandparents both died in the late 1980s, which gave me twenty-plus years of summers with them at the camp on Lockes Island at Lake Winnipesaukee; the same number of visits to the antebellum house on Allison Street in Concord, New Hampshire; and one memorable winter in Concord at Christmastime. There were at least vague years of interactions with my great grandmother and a few great uncles and aunts. There is also a vast collection of photographs that record the passing of time; summer after summer, the same yet changing family posing on the porch steps. I have had many opportunities since the 1970s to visit family at various times of the year.

Meanwhile, it might seem odd that a woman who enjoys warm weather and does not necessarily consider an icy day "delightfully bracing," would pine for a blustering, snowy walk in the afternoon, or a cool late summer day lazing in a rowboat, but there it is. The ancestors are calling; the glittery, rippling waters of Winnipesaukee are beckoning; and the voices of my mother, and those who came before her, are echoing across my soul.

When it gets quiet, my mind can conjure up the gentle whine and thud of the camp screen door; the slap of waves against the rocks; the rhythmic patter of rain on the tin roof. Remembering Concord, I can see my grandfather's massive garden filling up his Pleasant Street side yard. Inside the antebellum house the eclectic mix of Victorian and Arts and Crafts furniture are comfortably arranged from room to room. The old Victrola is waiting by the tall lace-curtained window for someone to wind it up. And in the quietest time of the night, that moment when everything else that is part of the day is set aside, I can still hear my grandparents talking together, their low voices murmuring, rumbling in the night like the last grumble of a faraway boat. It takes me back.

Spring

Spring

The birds came back.
The robins first,
And then the cardinals.
And soon the wood
was filled with chattering.
I had forgotten
just how deathly silent
winter is,
Until the birds came back.

Pilgrim Heart

He left all he had known,
Felt called
to seek a better world.
He never even owned a home,
But lived in temporary shelters,
Roaming place to place,
Sometimes a fertile field
to feed his soul,
Sometimes a barren ground
that scrubbed his heart with sand.
But all along,
He knew there was a future,
Something not yet seen,
A universe more sure,
More settled and secure
than what he had.
A city
whose foundations
came from God.
A promise
of a better country,
One that gave him holy steadiness
to overcome,
To manage day by day,
To loose the bonds of fear

SPRING—*PILGRIM HEART*

and restlessness that brought him down,
To know true peace,
Wherever,
And whenever should the curse be found.

Pilgrims

They came here
seeking someplace they could
build a life,
And freely worship God.
Though often faltering,
These trembling souls
were constantly enduring,
Leaning on their Father's arms,
And turning eager faces
toward the goal of their salvation.

Good fellows
on their journey into Promised Land,
They chose New Hampshire wilderness,
Strawbery Banke,
To be exact,
And settled there.
Steadfast,
Weary pilgrims,
Searching for some goodly place,
Some peace of heart,
While waiting for their final home.

Good fishing here,
Perhaps some profit-sharing

SPRING—*PILGRIMS*

with the English merchants,
Men already tethered to
the Maine—New Hampshire coast,
Men who boast about the furs,
The sassafras,
The fish.
Good earnings
for a man who has a family.

Still,
There is hard winter,
Cold that cuts across
the body and the soul.
Too many deaths,
Too many infants
buried with their elders,
Sleeping under heavy snows,
Joining others waiting while the winter blows.

Hard work.
Few words.

It is not fish,
Or sassafras
that holds the heart when winter comes,
But hope in God.
This is the wilderness,
And not the Promised Land,
They say,
And nod while salting down the cod.

MY MOTHER AND OTHER NEW ENGLANDERS

And we,
Descendants of their taciturn
and fierce tenacious spirits,
Carry on their work
of living day to day by grace.
We taste their hope.
We recognize
their testing and their trials,
Waiting,
Always waiting,
Comforted in life's extraordinary pain.
Like them,
A people with the sweetest longings,
Leaning forward in their restless expectations
of their final gain.

Going to Meeting

Come you pilgrims,
Call on God before your coming,
Sing the Psalms along the way.
Sing with grace,
And make sweet melody,
That all may taste and see
the Lord is good.
For He who knows our daily suffering,
Calls us each to bear our load.
We,
His troubadours of sorrow,
Walk as pilgrims on the royal road.
Each of us must make confession,
Each must ponder whose we are,
Each must contemplate our nature.
Who here comes,
Unless the Savior named our sin,
Yet drew us in,
And carried each of us thus far?

Find your narrow benches, sisters.
Brothers,
Rise to stand in prayer.
Let beauty rest upon this meeting,
Plain and simple is the dwelling,

MY MOTHER AND OTHER NEW ENGLANDERS

Filled with light,
His work revealed through people here.
Our hearts are shining,
Overwhelmed
by grace's fragrance everywhere.
The tender mercies of our Father
rest upon us
while we gather at Your table.
Lord, what a glorious sanctuary
from the tumult of this world!
He who saves us,
He who loves us,
Covers every thought and care.
Where else can eager pilgrims find
true courage in the time of struggle,
Strength to conquer grief and woe.
Come and join us at the altar,
Never falter.
He who heals
is He from whom all blessings flow.

Sorting

Sorting through old photographs,
Revisiting the paths
we took in other days,
I stop.

Remembering.

How long has passed
since I sat next to Walter?
Shared a custard cup with Grandma Kelly?
Played an old board game
and lost to Nana?
(Who could beat her?)
Listened shyly from the porch
to Gramps and Charlie
while they sipped Jack Daniels,
Trading quips and talking politics?
So long ago.
So far away.
Yet close enough for me
to give each picture shape,
And reignite a fading memory.

Ice-Out

Moan, lake, moan,
And groan away your crystal mantle,
Shake your shoulders,
Let your rippling muscles flow.
A thousand glistening, shivering slivers,
Glorious heaping frozen shards
that sing like tinkling bits of glass,
Are dancing,
Tumbling off your back.

We heard you grumble in your sleep.
The night is past,
So be awake.
For like some giant beast,
You have been too long fast asleep.
The dawn has come.
Come stir,
And be awake with me!
Come sing, lake, sing!
The sun is calling you to spring!

John's Ice-Out Recipe 1973–1983

You need an aluminum boat
and Merrill Fay,
To capture ice-out
on a day when foot-long shards
are gathering in bundles,
Tumbling
into icy stacks.
These are the facts:
Ram that boat up on the ice,
Then drag the craft,
And run across unstable floes,
Until your feet begin to sway,
And water seeps beneath your toes.
Then jump back in the boat
until you reach another glacial floe.
A daunting task,
I do agree.
But somehow you will get between
the island and the shore.

And why,
You ask,
Would someone race and skim the ice,
Would chance
an unexpected dip

MY MOTHER AND OTHER NEW ENGLANDERS

of dangerous proportions,
When,
Within another month,
The trip between the shore and island
could be happily accomplished,
And not become a cold,
Dramatic chore?

Why, indeed!
The ice, my friends,
The ice!
A marvelous wind
that whistles through a thousand sparkling shards
becomes an ecstasy of chimes!
A haunting, eerie song
that floats above the slippery floes,
And fills the air with music,
Canny, glorious melodies
that mark the end of winter's freeze,
The sleeping,
Seeping snow and silence that December brings.
These elegantly peculiar notes are singing change,
Their song replacing silent sleep
with timbrel's shivering crystals,
With the winds' own eager moans and creaks,
The waking sounds of coming spring.

Muddying

There is a tug of war
between
the winter and the spring,
Between
the dying and rebirth,
Between
our coming home,
And leaving earth,
When thawing fog
is dripping up above the snow,
And every corner of our lives
has turned to mud.
One day,
All cold and shivering packed into dirt—
A steady world beneath our feet,
The next,
All squishy,
Wet,
Unsettled ground and rising heat.
And then,
The cold again,
And all the contours we have labored to create,
Are frozen ruts to trip us up.

MY MOTHER AND OTHER NEW ENGLANDERS

It demonstrates our leaving,
All the struggle it has been,
And will be to the very end.
We live and die in muddying,
In fighting back against the melting snow,
In holding on to what we know
while praying eagerly for spring,
And all the while embracing cold.
Until one day
His promises
will truly melt away our messy muddiness.
And He Who Loves
us more than life,
Will take us home.

Sugar Maples in March

The maples shake off winter's chill,
Stretching,
Reaching branching arms
to feel the sun again,
Luxuriating in the pulse of life.
That sense that growing has begun,
Is filtering from short, brown buds,
Through chocolate-colored twigs,
Down to the trunk,
To stirring,
Hungry roots.
No leaves yet
on the trees.
But sap,
Grand, glorious sap
is rushing up to flood the limbs,
Coursing tendrilled branches,
Embracing swollen buds
where leaves will soon be breaking free.
The plastic pails are hanging,
Gathering a gallon here,
A gallon there.
It takes a lot of sap
to make a syrup from a tree.

Behold the Rain

Muggy.
Wet.
The moisture lingers
on my neck,
My shoulders,
Dripping down my back.
If only it would rain.

It will.

There are the signs—
Infant leaves are turning inward,
Cooler winds are flapping flags,
Gathering clouds are pushing back the sun,
And breezes sway the trees,
A constant rustling,
A restless energy
above a green and rolling bed of seas.
Hidden life is scurrying to find
where dry and shelter cover up
before a storm.
And something else is in the air—
A tense expectancy.
The hint of damp is everywhere.

SPRING—BEHOLD THE RAIN

It has begun.
What fun!
The greens are greener,
Browns,
More brown.
The sound!
The rhythmic,
Constant pattering,
The drum of rain on everything and everyone.
The eager leaves of trees and plants,
Their palms upturned
in hopes of catching every drop.
Cicadas all are silent.
Chattering insects dare not speak.
But hear the birds!
The birds are singing,
Laughing,
Calling to each other as they fly,
Who knew how thirsty
we have been!

Spider Hike

A web above me,
Almost invisible, if not for sun.
Big enough to catch a man,
I think.
And so I walk a widening arc
around this grand complexity,
This sticky net of dangers,
Silent,
Menacing.
Too bad I'm not
a spider whisperer,
A listener to arachnids
calling from their lacy bower.
What would they say
if they had wrapped me in
their withered room?
What have we trapped?
Or further still,
What has trapped us,
And broken down our velvet tomb?

New Baby 1929

She is a baby
bundled in a pram.
Another fading photograph,
A first-born
lavished on by mom and dad.
The scene,
The clothes
are 1929,
But this delightful print
is memory to anyone
who first discovered chubby cheeks,
Who counted tiny perfect toes
and smelled the sweetness in a newborn's hair.
And by their heir
have rediscovered their own selves,
A part of you and me
created into legacy,
A perpetuity of unknown possibilities.

Our life may falter,
Feel the fade.
(The photograph expresses
our diminished light.)
But this new infant
lifts our hopes.

MY MOTHER AND OTHER NEW ENGLANDERS

What wonders will this daughter do?
Is she like you?
She looks like me.

She Is an Artist

Drawing,
Always drawing.
Bits of colored pencils,
Charcoal,
Tubes of oil paints and watercolors,
Capturing the details of a world
just right outside my window,
Right outside the backyard fence,
Right outside the window of our car
as so much wonder races by,
Some close,
Some far.
Right outside the edges of the boat
that rumbles on its way to Camp,
Right outside the guardrails of the porch,
It does not matter where I am,
The birds,
The trees,
The very leaves,
The skies,
The water—
All these call to me to put it down on paper,
Recreate it with a palette knife,
Capture all the glories of my growing world,
The world I see before my searching and discerning eyes.

She Loves to Read

The *Book of Knowledge* is my friend.
From one end to the other,
I have read its contents:
Math and Science,
Words and Art,
A vast encyclopedic wonder
of the world I want to understand
and take apart.
Chapter after chapter,
Bringing
What's Out There into my room.
So many details to explore
and ponder on a rainy day,
So many possibilities to bring delight,
To understand a little more
about what's happening
beyond the door,
Beyond my neighborhood,
Beyond the edges that my family,
Oh, so carefully,
Have built
to bring protection to my life.
I'm pushing passed the boundaries of what I know.
How wonderful it is to lean
against the windowpane,

SPRING—*SHE LOVES TO READ*

And finally unpack.
So many tantalizing answers
to the questions I have asked.

She Is an Independent Woman

My father didn't hold
that girls should drive,
But I required steady transportation
back and forth from work.
And so, I bought a car,
A vintage 1939,
From Mr. Dick,
Who summered on the lake.
I paid him for the vehicle,
And he supplied *directionals*,
Front lights like giant googly eyes,
To let my fellow drivers know
just where my beautiful machine would go.

To Allison Street
my auto went,
While I set out to driving school
to learn the rules,
And how to make my old machine run respectfully.
A friend down from the lake
took me to Concord for my test.
I passed,
And drove the engine back.
I'd told my dad,
You see,

SPRING—SHE IS AN INDEPENDENT WOMAN

This grand machine belonged to me,
This car was mine to drive,
The driving one that he forbid.
And I would move it
from its driveway spot
when I could do it by myself.
And so, I did.

Her Name Is Music

When I was growing up,
In summer
I would lie upon my bed upstairs
and listen to the waves
that splashed against the rocks,
Listen to the thunder
as it rolled across the sky,
Listen to the rhythmic drumming
of the rain across a metal roof,
Listen to the rumbling boats
that echoed up and down the lake,
Listen to the sound of people's voices
murmuring in conversation as they wandered by.
I heard the music of the lake.

When I was growing up,
My mother walked me
to a teacher,
Someone to initiate in eager fingers
all the mysteries
of our old upright,
An instrument hauled up the backside of the house
and through a second-story window.
I would practice daily scales,
And listen to ascending and descending notes

that skipped and sometimes stumbled up and down the stairs,
And listen as the scales became a melody of memory
that turned in time
to intricacies of harmonies,
Of patterns, and of chords.
And as my fingers felt their way along,
I heard the music of the song.

When I was growing up,
I joined the *Junior Music Club,*
And ushered,
In a formal gown,
Inviting others in to hear
the graciousness of sound performed,
A theater of singing on the stage,
Both secular and sacred choral works,
Some soloists unknown,
And some renowned,
And listen to the way that music
filled the hall and heart with energies and colored pictures,
Images and textures all around.
I heard the music as an art.

When I was growing up,
I did not know that someday I would play
for my own growing girls,
Or share a life with someone
who had heard the music just like me,
Or live among the melodies that daily filtered
through the air we breathed.

MY MOTHER AND OTHER NEW ENGLANDERS

But there you see,
From early on,
I heard the music speak,
And it found me.

Sugar Hill in June

If lupine flourishes
in drouth
as Frost implies,
Then such a canopy of flowers
should be much admired.
Who would think
such bountiful arrays
would drink much less
than any other eager sprays of beauty
filling up the pastures and the fields?
Sweet nature yields a panoply of spiky wonders,
Tall and gloriously majestic
in their purples,
Pinks,
Their whites and blues,
With underlying leaves,
A circular explosion
shooting lancet spikes like tiny fireworks!

It feeds my heart.

For it is truly art that celebrates that spring has come!
And boldly where I look,
The meadows sing and laugh at me
for settling,

MY MOTHER AND OTHER NEW ENGLANDERS

Expecting lesser grace,
A flower here,
A flower there.

This grand exuberance,
This lavish loving on display
by Him who made it all,
Reminds this mindful passerby that His creation never skimps.
And I am left to stand in awe.
Behold His banquet
spread before my eyes!
A savoring of light and color everywhere I glimpse!

Petal Snow

Petal snow
falls down
in flurries,
Pink and white
descending,
Dancing,
Swirling,
Blowing.
Yesterday
their fragrant pieces
dressed a tree.

Summer

Summer Is

Summer
is learning on the fly,
Hands on,
Fingers running through the dirt,
Barefoot,
Tennis shoes without the socks,
Living out-of-doors
from waking sun
to fading light.
Fishing,
Hiking,
Swimming,
Sitting on the shore,
And watching
endless rippling waters pour and splash
against the rocks.

Summer

Green,
There's so much green!
Bright Life is running,
Upward,
Up from dirt and earth and soil,
Greenness saturating all around,
A living canvas,
Overflowing human spaces,
Gobbling up directed places,
Eradicating borders,
Fences,
Who can possibly bring order
when the grasping,
Lapping edges of creation keep on growing?

And all about
the forest floor,
A vivid,
Tousled shag
of ivy,
Mixed with moss and stick.
A woven lawn,
Its elements all reaching hungrily for glints of sun
that dance and fly between
the rippling canopy of trees,

SUMMER—*SUMMER*

Their leaves and branches
like a thousand clapping hands
of summer fun.

Through musty layers,
(Life is breathing)
Smells rush up,
The air is dank and moldy,
Heat and cool all mixed.
Decaying underbrush is feeding nascent life,
Debris is making pablum for another tree,
A budding grass,
A fledgling bush.
And oh, the smell of it!
The heady fragrance of vitality!

Skunk Trouble 1915

We used to summer up on Meredith Neck,
Looking down to view Lockes Island
by the Witches.
We used to go and visit,
But we wanted our own camp.
So, when the ice went out,
Dad reconnected with the family that owned the place.
Otis went to school with Dad,
And they were awfully glad to see each other once again,
Otis being interested in selling us a space.

Discussion,
Picked a lot,
Bought.

So, John Cate,
(Mother's brother) and his sons,
And my own brother, Walter,
Went up to our spot and pitched a tent.
They built the Camp.
They worked long hours, I expect.
And in the process,
Some made note there was a skunk about.

SUMMER—SKUNK TROUBLE 1915

Mother used to go up once a week.
She'd cook the meals,
And store them in old fashioned trunks.
One day she'd come to do some good,
And when they went to bed,
They didn't shut the cover to the trunk.
The skunk got in and spoiled food.

Another night,
My uncle shoved my brother's arm
to wake him up.
For Gosh sakes, Walter,
Whispered John,
Don't move!
For there,
Between the two,
Too busy shuffling,
Wandering back and forth inside the tent,
The animal was checking out the sparse accommodations,
Trying to decide just why he came.
And finally, his curiosity was satisfied
that there was nothing worth remembering,
And so, he left.

My uncle and the others thought it best
to trap the skunk.
And in the morning,
Uncle John discovered Mr. Skunk inside the box.
He let him go.
The others rushed about,

MY MOTHER AND OTHER NEW ENGLANDERS

Expecting there to be an eager critter caught inside the trap,
But he was gone.
And Uncle John remarked,
He had been neatly captured,
But,
He only left a calling card!

Temptation

It's early June.
The ice went out in May
this year.
And all the sparkling water beckons me.

Too soon to swim, I think.

Between the ice and natural underwater springs,
This glacial lake
would feel like liquid snow.
A wonder to amaze
and tantalize,
But far too brisk.
So clean,
So clear,
It calls to me
to let my hand create a wandering wake,
And push this liquid snow about.
I might give in.
There is that risk,
That what drips through my fingers
might be good enough to splash,
Or maybe cool the sun
that warms my neck.

MY MOTHER AND OTHER NEW ENGLANDERS

Too cold.

But still I drift.
I'm thinking strongly about testing silver water
on an early summer's day.

Okay.

And so I go,
Screaming,
Yelling off the dock!
The shock of liquid snow
assails my every pore.
I cannot breathe.
And then for sixty staggering seconds
I adore the view—
The water up around my chin,
The maddening paddling
before the chattering sets in,
Before my freezing lips turn blue.
A towel, please,
For goodness' sake.
But oh,
The joy,
The glorious joy of racing out into the lake!

John's Boats

A man needs a boat
when he lives on the lake.
My first was a Laker,
Bought 1919.
Originally built for Lakeport's mayor,
She was christened *Thetis,*
Mother of Achilles,
Daughter of the sea.
She was long and lean
with a five-foot beam.

Uncle Levi,
Later on,
Replaced her motor—
A new car engine.
It gave her a growl,
And an elegant sputter,
She rumbled and puttered from island to shore.
She stayed afloat for thirty years more.

In '67,
I discovered rot.
It was not enough to clean the wound.
It was not enough to wash,

MY MOTHER AND OTHER NEW ENGLANDERS

To sand,
To paint her bright.
For fifty-two years she carried the crew.
This grand old lady
had served us well.
But I must be frank.
We took her to Fay's,
And there she sank.

The next boat,
Known as *Baker's Boat*,
Was built on Long Island
from cypress planks,
Which work just fine
as long as the boat is always asea.
But being drydocked over winter months,
The planks dry out.
Which means every spring,
She was put on lifters
to ease her slowly back into the deep,
To make her swell,
And end the shrink.
With this minor kink
she was prone to leaks,
And anyone taking a ride would tell
they were primed and ready to bail or sink.

My third boat,
Built in '76,

SUMMER—JOHN'S BOATS

By Seaway Boats,
Was made in Maine.
They finished the hull,
And had it sent to Fay's Boatyard
where Merrill put the engine in.
A marvelous craft,
Built of excellent wood and fiberglass.
The *Thetis II*
has had some repairs,
And her overhauls for wear and tear.
But she perseveres.
She is still afloat after forty years.
She serves my son,
And his son, too.

For one hundred-plus years
there has been a boat
to ferry us back and forth to Camp—
To deliver the groceries
and pick up mail,
To transport family coming to stay
for weekend fishing,
For leisurely checking on neighbors nearby,
For afternoon driving across the lake.
From year to year,
Through every day,
These ladies were faithful around the clock.
And here on the porch,
As I reminisce,

MY MOTHER AND OTHER NEW ENGLANDERS

I still enjoy
the rumbling motor,
The feel of the wind and spray on my face,
And the quiet bump,
As a wake knocks the hull against the dock.

Blueberry Picking with Nancy

The Shakers made good neighbors,
Taking in a host of orphans,
Giving them a gentle home.
And all the Cates,
Those twelve or more rambunctious children,
Thought the Shaker orphans
excellent companions,
Friends to play with at the farm.
Great berry pickers all,
They gathered scores of bright blueberries
from the bushes taller than a standing man
that grew amid the boggy brush
of fertile Broken Ground,
Where all the most delicious berries could be found.
And so the Cates and Shaker children flourished,
Nourished by believing
in the simple gifts between good friends,
Earnestly,
And in accord,
That all the time God gave
was His own gift to them,
And how they used the time allowed
was their own gifting back to Him,
And what was worked or made by hands
could easily be shared.

MY MOTHER AND OTHER NEW ENGLANDERS

One family in the world,
But never truly of it,
Found the others
who were seeking to shake off the sin that hindered.
Here they met together in a boggy field
to pick sweet berries,
Looking for community,
For opportunity to tender grace.
And there,
Among the picking,
All the chattering and giggles,
Conversations galloping from thought to racing thought,
The children sought
and celebrated
all the cheerfulness they dared
that usually accompanies when goodly,
Never-ending friendship is declared.

Traveling

It takes all day to get there.
Five girls packed like sardines
in an aging car,
A station wagon
loaded up with snacks,
With blankets,
And with pillows,
Captures eager faces,
Faces searching out familiar landmarks
that appear along the road.

It takes too long
as we move deftly
in between the trucks that own the route.
Are we inside the bridge,
Or up above?
And New York City passes by,
The cityscapes becoming miles and miles
of road and trees.

And then Connecticut,
The state that lasts forever.
Time to count the cows or take a nap,
Refold the map,

MY MOTHER AND OTHER NEW ENGLANDERS

Tell a story,
Anything but think about how long it takes.
At last the entrance into Massachusetts.
Gaining, gaining ground,
Closer—
Are we there yet?
Many voices ask again,
Positions shift,
Elusive efforts to explore a softer seat
while cracker crumbs adorn the floor
beneath our feet.

Quite suddenly,
The pines of Massachusetts
melt away to glorious birch,
White paper birch
all crowded in groves
by granite boulders.
It is as if the glacier
clawed the ground,
Then lifted hills,
No sense of order in these brazen mounds,
And threw the granite back to fill the gaps.
Roll down the windows!
Smell the air!
We're getting there!
Why does it always take so long?

Nashua,
Then Merrimack.

SUMMER—TRAVELING

At last!

The Concord House.

We eat and sleep downstairs.

The floorboards creak,

The tall Victorian windows gather sun,

Their steadfast glory only kept at bay by shades.

There is a dark patina left by use and age

on everything—

The well-worn polished wood

where many hands have brushed across

the rails that decorate the stairs,

The solitary bulbs

that hang from heights,

Long pendulums of light

with even longer chains,

The sense of conversations,

Whispers,

Pauses,

Words of love and life

still lingering,

Their stories burnished into all the elements of house and home.

The ticking clocks,

The sense of time slowed down.

The sense that sometimes long is good,

That waiting can be filled with grace,

A place to savor slow instead of hurrying,

To rediscover time as friend,

MY MOTHER AND OTHER NEW ENGLANDERS

To see,
At least a little while,
Those spaces of eternity
that fill and overflow the edges of our finite world.
Are we there yet?

Dockside

The water,
Playfully
is nudging dock,
Is catching all the glints of sun
and tossing them like fairy dust upon the shore.
As other boats go by,
Each passing swell
bumps up against the hull.
The ropes are tugging,
Whining,
As the craft is pulled from side to side.
And *Thetis* groans to hear
some water sprite
has asked if this boat could come out and play.
Cool ripples tease and shove,
The vessel deftly rocked.
It wants to nose its bow into the spray.
Instead,
It stays.
This is the time to sleep,
To hug the dock.
And so it sits and sighs,
Still straining on its mooring lines.

Stone on Stone

He built a wall.
Laid stone on stone
to shelter in a wharf,
To keep the ice at bay
where winters often crumple lesser docks,
To keep the waves from buffeting,
From wearing down his summer boat.
This dock would stand alone when others buckled in the cold
and were replaced from year to year.
This dock would hunker down,
Would stand against the eastern breeze
that slammed both boat and waves into the pier.
This dock would soldier on.
Such steadiness,
Such permanence of stone,
Of one man's quarrel
with the endless elements of change,
Would hold the wood,
Restrain the water fast.
This dock would last.

And so it did.
This man believed he was the stone,
And waves were minor adversaries
if a man could bail.

SUMMER—STONE ON STONE

He did not even learn to swim,
Depending on his sturdy boat
and years of skill.
And he believed the woman would be there,
Just like his boat,
One stone beside another,
Firmly placed,
A wall against
whatever life could throw their way.

And then she wasn't.
Wasn't wandering about before the dawn.
Wasn't chiding him for speaking out of turn.
Wasn't reading her devotions,
Every word she spoke aloud
a sweet reminder of her gentleness and grace.
Wasn't there to be his wall,
The fortress he'd depended on for all their married life.
He hadn't known his wall was her
until she slipped away,
Awakening to better worlds.
She'd been the wall between his heart
and all the waves that always rolled and rippled there.
She'd been the boat that kept him steady,
Even when the bilges took on water,
Knocking hard against the dock.
She'd been his rock,
The stone on stone
that sheltered him from day to day,
From year to year.

And one small dock,
Protected by a rugged wall,
The one he thought displayed
his sternest self,
His Yankee ingenuity at play,
Expressed more keenly than a thousand words
could ever say,
What this man's woman did for him,
So quietly and tenderly behind the scenes,
From early light to end of day.

Memories

Lived here all your life?
I ask,
Not yet,
He says,
And we both laugh.
Old jokes seem fresh
when they are shared with friends,
With people we have known and loved for many years.
My thoughts are now just memories.
But gentle conversations
between John and me,
Between my grandfather
and his daughter's girl,
Still take me back
to catching perch out in the boat,
To sitting on the porch
as casting shadows slowly turn
our scene of endless water
into sounds that fill the spaces in the dark—
The noisy slaps of errant waves against the rocks,
The screen door's groan and slam
as people wander in and out,
In and out,
The muffled roar of speedboats out beyond our view,
Their motors echoing across the lake.

MY MOTHER AND OTHER NEW ENGLANDERS

The smells of supper linger,
Moving camp to camp along the breeze.
Tonight we eat the fish we caught,
And I am thankful to be brought again
to have these memories fulfilled just one more time.
A crowd of bugs fly suddenly
into the zapper hanging on a tree,
And we enjoy a glorious burst of sparks,
Another joke that we can share.
Some summer fireworks, he says,
Before we head into the Camp
to eat the supper waiting there.

Life with John

We'd been to shore
in *Baker's Boat*,
Too early in the summer
for this craft to float
without some time to swell.
It took on water.
Not enough at first to notice
more than normal leaking in the bilge,
But as we closed in on Lockes Island,
It became apparent
(Water up above our ankles,
Making headway toward our knees)
that John would have to guide this sinker
in between the docks.

Indeed, he did.
We made it safely to the rocks
before the vessel settled on the bottom,
Water now up to our waist.
Full water-logged,
And feeling early summer's windy draft.
We headed home,
And left to Merrill Fay
to do the job of rescuing our soggy craft.

MY MOTHER AND OTHER NEW ENGLANDERS

It was a while before we ventured back to town.
And John,
Who never learned to swim,
Was philosophical about the whole event,
A Yankee always confident,
Replied when asked,
On whether he was ever worried or afraid,
Said,
Everything is fine,
As I am sure that anyone who has been born to hang,
Will never drown.

Fishing Therapy

Lake trout takes live bait,
He tells me,
Salmon like to nip at flies.

Fishing is for sitting,
Waiting,
Listening to the waves lap at the hull,
And hearing cries of birds as they go by.
Fishing is for feeling rested
while this vessel gently rocks us,
Dipping,
Rolling,
Sun surrounding,
Warming up our backs and faces.

Sure would like to reel some supper in.

Shhh,
He whispers.
It's so silent in this sitting,
Even hums of motors seem quite far away,
Their distant echoes
rumble quietly across the lake,
Like passing thunder coming from some lost forgotten storm
left over from another shore.

MY MOTHER AND OTHER NEW ENGLANDERS

Not even traces
of such weather here.
We check our lines.
Looks like no one's home today.

Milkman

I remember
(I am talking with my mother)
when the milkman traveled
porch to porch,
The metal insulated box
that graced our narrow stoop,
The rattling clink of glass,
Glass bottles,
Shuffling,
Gently bumping with each other,
Here I pause.
A lovely sound,
I say and sigh.
My mother smiles.
Her memories go farther back than mine,
Another milk delivery
when she had been the girl instead of me.
Refrigeration didn't come to Camp for many years,
She says,
Warming up to tell her tale.
No lights,
No grand electric anything.
She casually continues from remembering.
We had a milkman, too.
We had two great big ice chests on the porch,

MY MOTHER AND OTHER NEW ENGLANDERS

And Mr. Bates brought us our milk and ice.

Now harvesting this grand commodity,
This winter ice for summer's play,
Requires understanding when to cut the ice,
And where to keep it safely cold.
Customers will soon be looking for effective ways to keep their dairy fresh.
From ice-in to ice-out
was the phrase that marked the days.
They figured out
the perfect time for harvesting.
Ice-in is when the lake is frozen shore to shore,
Ice-out is when the Mount is able
once again to get to all her ports of call.

They'd clean the snow,
Chart a grid,
Then cut the blocks
and move 200 tons of cold out off the lake
to icehouses situated all along the shore,
Where freezing blocks were packed in sawdust,
Waiting for the heat,
For summer cottages to bring demand,
And keep these winter/summer businesses afloat.
Your milkman came by truck.
Mine came by boat.

And I keep thinking
of the ice chest up at Camp,

SUMMER—*MILKMAN*

The one beneath the window in the kitchen,
Where my Nana kept the bread and cheese.
I still remember
looking for the cord that wasn't anywhere,
And wondering
just how they ever kept it cold,
And why they needed it
when on the other wall,
Beside the sink,
There was a working,
White refrigerator standing there!
And then I pause again.
My mother's musing thoughts have truly passed a torch.
Her memory,
A remnant of another life before my time,
Has passed to me,
For I am also just a remnant of another memory.
My children never will experience
a milk box on the family stoop.
I am its final resting place,
The last reiteration of an icebox on the porch.

Boat Errands 1960s

"Goin' to shore,"
John calls out generously,
So everyone can hear.
"Got any takers?"
His son-in-law obliges,
Thinking he could take
the car up to the Star for eggs and such.
"And here's the trash,"
Adds Nettie,
Handing John a bag.
Granddaughter Sheila wants to come.
Still so young.
Almost ten.
But she is hoping for adventure,
Already reaching for the trash,
Life jacket in her other hand
to look the part of indispensable
before her father might say no.

She was the one
to go to shore in restless wind and rain
last summer.
Waves were rocking Grandpa's sturdy craft
from side to side,
Some water sloshing in the bilge.

SUMMER—BOAT ERRANDS 1960S

Sheila isn't one to be afraid.
She doesn't mind.
She knows old wooden boats
all take a while each spring to swell
before the leaking stops.
The boards are fitted tight,
Both fore and aft by hot July,
But Sylvia's clan are always at the lake in June,
The cooler, wetter time.
Too soon for fitted tight.
So anyone who grabs a ride,
Had better be prepared to bail.

The three amigos hurry to the dock.
They loose the mooring lines.
"Don't forget the mail,"
My mother calls out from the porch,
And off the boat is running,
Grumbling motor
wheezing,
Coughing,
Rumbling,
Smells of diesel
in the blowing mists of heavy bubbles in the lake.
The hint of some adventure waiting to be found,
The swelling ancient creature creaks as rolling waves push hard
    against the hull.

MY MOTHER AND OTHER NEW ENGLANDERS

Too tired now,
Too old today, it seems to say,
But out they go into the lake,
And on to town.

John's Fireworks 1940s

What is a glorious Fourth
without some noise?
If local children were allowed,
I'd let them watch me
shooting color-coded lightning in the air.
A loud,
Delightful day!

One year,
A parent said *no more*,
And I was told to put my fireworks away.
A Yankee,
A resourceful creature,
Doesn't let somebody's *no*
stand in the way of fun,
And so I called on Morris,
He who knew his dynamite,
To turn an ordinary display
into something eminently practical.
The dynamite would make the necessary noise,
And crush the rocks.
The crush would level ground above the Camp for basketball.
One stick of dynamite,
Plus mud,
And one good blasting cap,

And boom!
Our fireworks were done.

One year,
He and his son came out,
And planted ten sticks over one huge rock.
There was a grand,
Humongous roar,
And thundering like we had never heard before,
And what was left of rock?
No pieces bigger than a hand.
A perfect celebration that a Yankee mind can plan!
What is a glorious Fourth
without some noise?

John's Garden

Mistah Maynard,
Says the tall boy at the door,
Can I have your rhubab, please?
Grandpa nods,
And I watch,
As the boy breaks off a stalk,
And eats it raw!
I cannot help but make a sour face.
How can he choose such bitter vegetables
to nibble on,
And why does Grandpa even give them space?

But here it is,
His Victory Garden,
Borne of other wars and times,
When all commercial crops
were going overseas to feed the troops,
And trains and trucks
were busy hauling Army food
instead of local vegetables and fruits.

Sow the seeds of victory,
They advertised in World War I.
Stretch your ration coupons,
Was the tag in World War II.

John lived through both.
And sometime in between,
Perhaps when food was getting scarce,
While one calamity was folding hard into another,
John got patriotic,
Sowing seeds for beans and beets,
For cabbages and carrots,
Lettuce,
Turnip greens and peas,
The tasty delicacies that feed a hungry family
from the summer on through rationing,
When worlds of worrying keep on coming from the front,
When what the Army does is never quite enough,
And the threat of Hitler getting close
can take the savor out of ordinary stuff.

It leaves a tired heart in dread.

So why not raise a bed of joy,
A garden to move hopeless from today?
This unsafe world would fade away
when John reached down to pull the carrots from the dirt,
And pick the freshest cabbages for Nettie's tasty stew.
He loved the work of growing crops on his own private land,
Or watch while Nettie turned his produce
into food between them,
Cooked, and saved, and canned.

John also raised a thousand different gladiolas.
They took the beds for vegetables,

SUMMER—JOHN'S GARDEN

And added color to the place.
He used to dig them up before the frost,
To sleep inside until their time in spring.
He wanted color, fully dressed.
(He added peonies,
Some lilacs, and some roses in to fill the rest.)

I do not know how much John understood,
Or knew his garden spoke of greater truth—
The lilacs and the peonies as harbingers of hope,
Of great beginnings still to come,
Their very glory claiming that a broken universe
could leave the dark,
Become undone.
His roses,
Lilacs,
All his gladiolas
witnessed day by day,
As neighbors,
All exclaiming,
Wandered passed,
Admiring the gardener's art—
That they were grand observers
of a Gardening,
A mending far more gracious than a human task,
And He who made it all
would guarantee that
Life would last.

Timber Blues

Trees would crawl across the road
if not for cars.
Even so,
I see their branches waving to each other,
Branches reaching out across both sides
of tarred and painted lanes,
Their roots all eagerly in forward motion,
Growing out, not only down.
If they could only breach the paths that separate
one cousin from another.

On some back roads,
Limbs and branches almost make a tunnel,
Branch by branch,
So close,
Yet never close enough.
For hard machines keep rolling down,
A constant flow,
And so the walls of green and brown
keep growing,
Leaning,
Never yielding,
Rustling,
Murmuring,
While waving boughs move endlessly

SUMMER—TIMBER BLUES

to reestablish contact lost,
Working furiously at growing,
Spreading,
Reaching toward elusive sky
while bending toward each other's grasp.
And they would take the land between them back,
If not for all the noisy metal,
Rushing,
Rattling,
Racing past.

Summer Life

I hear the growling mowers
cutting,
Long before their fragrant
mix of gas and greenness
filters through my bedroom window
on a warming breeze.
Early sun devours all the waning shadows
in my room.
Good time to be awake
and out the door.
Good time to go explore,
Bring high adventure down the street
and through the woods.
Good time to run,
To bike,
To roller skate.
You must not hesitate.
Go out and seek another hike,
Another game or two,
At least until the evening's growing darkness
scatters,
Smudges out today.
Such lack of light,
Too soon will bring imagination down to size,
But not before I dance among the fireflies.

Autumn

Autumn

I like the yellow,
Red,
And purple hues.
Creation trying out a different dress.
If only it would last.
But all that vibrant color
tells me trees are only shedding summer clothes,
Maples,
Oaks,
And other folks
discarding last year's finery
for snowy heavy overcoats.
What looked at first like something new
is only old and rapidly becoming raw,
And I am left to rake away
the tattered remnants
of their last hurrah.

Changing Weather

Winds are blowing,
Heady winds.
The end of somnolence
and solitude
is giving way to schedule and care.
No more long afternoons at play,
No sun to warm our backs
as we roam centuries,
High adventurers exploring future
grand imaginations,
Bringing everything to present.
Now,
Tomorrow seems so far away,
So far from growing old.
Now and then will find itself,
And we'll be waiting there.
Expectant,
Energized and rested,
Eagerly we'll test another day.
But here it is—
The briskness blowing through,
Cool winds of change,
The reds and yellows making
secret streaks and edges under all the leaves.

AUTUMN—CHANGING WEATHER

I will adjust.
I always do.
I'll find a joy in cold and brilliant-colored trees.
But for today,
For now,
I will look back
and feed the fading warmth,
Remembering what once was there.
I'll grieve a summer lost
for just today,
That sense of growing old,
And then I'll walk out into autumn,
Deeply breathe its energies,
Embracing cold.

First Blush

When autumn starts,
It hesitates to change.
It took a wet and sturdy spring
to bring the leaves and flowers in,
And summer grew the leaves
so generously broad and full,
It seems a waste to drop them all
on someone's yard.
But here we are,
Already testing out new shades—
Rum raisin,
Violet and butterscotch,
Warm rust and carmine,
Tangerine and amber,
Almost anything will do but green.
A fringe of red that decorates,
A climbing trunk
with yellow ruffled hair.
It hasn't quite yet
turned into the flush of brilliant colors
soon to be displayed,
But it will come.
And every tree will blush with vibrancy,
At least a week or more,
Before,

AUTUMN—*FIRST BLUSH*

Well-winded,
Every branch will shake off
every leaf,
Too tired to maintain
such finery another day.
Those well-dressed trees are sure that
Truly none have been arrayed
as fine as us,
And thus we are too drained and sleepy
to remain another moment with this modeling.
We are fatigued,
They'd say,
If they could speak.
We need a rest,
But we'll be back
with new couture in early spring.

Change

Brisk weather,
And the days are waning,
Folding up their long and hectic summer zest
for quieter,
More contemplative rest.
But long before the need
to rearrange the blankets on the bed,
Or pack the summer clothes away,
There are more walks,
More complimenting on the splash of colors
peeking out among the leaves of green,
More noticing that change is also in the air,
That what is seen,
That sense of slowing down,
Is hiding all the grand activity
just out of sight,
Above me,
And around.
I notice squirrels are rushing everywhere,
Dashing up the trees,
And underfoot along the ground.

Huskin' Party 1896–1902

I was a boy,
He said,
His story fading into yesterday,
And we both let his memories
rise up to play.
They planted corn,
He recollects,
His mother's world before his eyes.
And Mother's sister went around
to put some red ears here and there amid the rows.
The corn grew tall,
Was harvested.
They pulled it off the stocks
and made a big pile in the barn.
Then people gathered,
Neighbors who had heard
there was a huskin' at the Oak Hill Farm.
They all sat down
and husked that corn,
Then piled it neatly,
Ready for the reveling.
For any man who found and kept a red ear,
Could accept a stolen kiss.
And any miss who could be caught,
She ought to let him place at least one peck upon her cheek.

MY MOTHER AND OTHER NEW ENGLANDERS

One man thought his red ear
gave him pass to chase and smooch with every lass.
At least that's what I'm told.
I wasn't old enough to really know.

And so,
The chasing ended up
with setting down to oyster stew,
Until the Fiddle Man got up to play,
And everybody danced away
their tired backs,
The grand monotony of every day,
The disappointments when the crop was sparse,
The lack of rain,
Or too much snow,
When wintertime refused to go.

The hope of harvest
stacked up neatly in the barn,
Reminding them that they could trust in
what God gave,
And what they knew,
Reviving even weary folks
to carry on another year.
And here,
He turned to me and said,
I went to bed.
That's all I know about a huskin'.

Good Cider

Cool,
Sweet cider.
Bracing,
Always tasty,
Delightfully refreshing cider.
It settled in the East
and spanned the prairie,
Gave us all a way to keep things merry,
Quenched our thirst
and rallied troops at the Battle of Concord,
Fueled fresh politicking and gathering,
Got some presidents elected,
Made for drinking and enjoying,
Always part of patriotic celebrations,
It was front and center for this country's farming operations.

Now I,
Reflecting on the old stone house,
I do recall a cider mill,
A wooden building
hitched right to the farmhouse wall.
It had a box to put the apples in.
A piece of tin
with nails to grind the apples up.
They used a horse to turn the wheel

MY MOTHER AND OTHER NEW ENGLANDERS

that moved the cogs,
And ground the apples into mush.
I wasn't old enough
to do much more than lead the horse.
The work was something for a boy to do
to keep him out of scrapes and such.
It was a job,
An afternoon of proper work
out on the farm.
It kept us busy fellows near the folks and out of harm.

Much later still,
When Mother's brother John
would work his cider wonders at the mill in Concord,
I took my children with their jugs
to fill their cups with cider.

Choice of Jefferson and Adams,
More for presidents than kings.
Much more glorious than any other beverages
now served,
As far back now as I can recollect or think,
It still remains the most delightfully refreshing,
Sweet and tasty,
Always bracing drink.

Cranberry Time at the Old Stone House

Beside the house
was a meadow place,
And a kind of bog.
The folks grew cranberries in that sog.
In the fall,
They would dam the water
clear under the bridge,
Get the cranberries covered,
And pick as many as they could hold.
Then when winter came,
They'd skate on the ice
until early spring.
When the dam was opened,
The water run out,
A boy could go picking the cranberries about.

Now this berry is known
to be good as a juice,
A good sweetener, too.
And now at Thanksgiving,
A relish or sauce.
But a boy out picking
is never at loss
to leave some in his pail,
Keep some in his hand.

MY MOTHER AND OTHER NEW ENGLANDERS

To savor the flavor,
He'd hold by a few,
Leaving some for the sauces,
And the rest,
A good chew.

Leftovers

My mother came from leaner times,
Depression times
that filled her daily life with making do,
With using what she had.
You'd think that managing without
might give my mother discontent,
But you'd be wrong.
Instead,
It taught her to respect
the lost potentials any item could possess.
Two printed sacks could be a dress.
The fat drained from the Sunday beef or pork—
The makings for some bars of soap.
A piece of paper,
(With some bits of glue)—
An envelope.
While very young,
Her eyes were trained
to see the possibilities each item could produce.
And so she turned some remnant eyelet fabric
(From a wedding)
into curtains for the window in the powder room.
While learning how to stitch a winter coat,
She figured just enough material to make one for herself,
A matching version for her youngest girl.

MY MOTHER AND OTHER NEW ENGLANDERS

This world ignores its leftovers,
Their fragments often tossed aside,
The dubs and drabs
that seems too useless to consider any other use.
But she would disagree.
Leftovers come with hidden joys,
Creative avenues and new directions,
Treasures waiting to be found.
For long ago she learned to seek the unexpected
in the leftovers that came around.

Good Flavors

A kitchen is a wondrous place
when there are cooks about.
I am not one of them.
I have a penchant more for writing,
More for teaching
than for culinary chemistry.
But those who naturally
make music out of food,
My grandmother,
My mother,
These two have brought my palate into harmony
with oh so many flavorful delights,
That to this day,
When I remember dandelion greens,
Or succotash,
Or pudding with dollops of cold ice cream,
I think of them,
I think of home.

My mother doesn't do much cooking anymore.
She still makes chowder, though.
And if I'm in her house
to see and smell the bubbling liquid
with its bits of fish,
I am transported back to

MY MOTHER AND OTHER NEW ENGLANDERS

her own mother's Concord kitchen.
I am there.
I see my Nana sitting on her stool before the stove,
Creating warm deliciousness with fish,
And milk,
And salted pork.
My memories of Nana often scurry after something good to eat.

She was the first to introduce my stomach
to the wide varieties of sweet—
The mildly, creamy sweet of lobster roll,
The heavy, chewy sweet molasses flavor
in a Hermit after lunch,
The punch of satisfaction
when the tongue uncovers sweet is meeting tartness
in strawberry-rhubarb pie.
I like them all.

And in the fall,
I still remember my own mother
stirring up sweet Boston baked beans,
Ingredients and recipes passed down
from mother down to mother,
All their goodness simmering
within the pot,
The aromatic artistry of beans,
Of sweet molasses,
And of salted pork.
How wonderful to savor their shared cooking ingenuity
with homemade brown bread slices,

AUTUMN—GOOD FLAVORS

Little bits of butter spread quite thinly on the top.
These flavors I remember
still in memory are melting in my mouth,
The taste of love,
The work,
Somedays the sheer monotony that went into a host
of daily baking,
Broiling,
Boiling,
Roasting,
Steaming,
Making something wonderful with simple foods,
Is what my heart remembers most.

Leaf Peeping Along the Kanc

It rained here yesterday,
Which darkened up the bark,
And washed the dirt away.
The leaves are bright,
And sunlight only emphasizes color
sponged across the hillsides
like a pointillism smudge of
miles and miles of autumn's royal splendor.
All the trees have shaken out their formal wear
in rich vermillion,
Dandelion yellow,
Tangerine and pumpkin orange,
Some surprising spots
in deepest plum.
The trees remaining green look plain
beside their brilliant neighbors,
Ordinary,
Dressed for summer, not for fall,
As if they missed the memo sent to all.

The falling leaves are everywhere.
I feel a crispness in the air
as breezes lift and swirl the color
freed from limbs and branches overhead.
These ride a symphony of dances,

AUTUMN—LEAF PEEPING ALONG THE KANC

A vibrant color storm that falls and twirls
like errant snow,
And settles aimlessly around the forest floor.

Such glory is not silent beauty,
Rather sound on sound.
This colored carpet,
All too soon,
Will turn to brown,
A crunching,
Crinkling music underfoot.
But now the sounds of river water,
Splashing,
Surging madly over rocks and boulders,
Rubbing shoulders with the edges of the bank,
Reflects the laughter in the air,
The joyous vividness,
The flashy,
Almost gaudiness of color reaching out to capture every possible display,
Reverberating,
Kaleidoscopic richness overflowing,
Celebrating,
That the end of hot and languid summer
finally has ushered in
the longer, cooler night,
And bracing,
Meant for harvesting,
More energetic day.

Autumn Breeze

Cold wind is wild today,
Blowing,
Throwing,
Scolding up the piles
of long-forgotten leaves
in overflowing handfuls.
Suddenly,
It tosses high
a torrent of old fading colors,
Colors flying,
Falling,
Lifting,
Skittering and dancing
on their edges,
Racing with each other,
Riding reckless breaths of air.
All the while,
These elements of trees
are scattering quite effortlessly
about the street.
And I am captured,
Caught inside this wondrous whirl
of restless autumn breeze.
Wind, blow,

AUTUMN—*AUTUMN BREEZE*

I say,
And cover me with leaves!

On Hurricanes

It came in bellowing in '38,
Unruly,
Screeching,
Moaning winds,
A bellyache of noise and fuss.
It had been flooding other towns,
Consuming property and house,
Dismantling livelihoods
in other states.
I heard New Bedford and Long Island
both were drowning in its stormy surge.
Here in town,
The Merrimack came up
and scoured through the thoroughfares.
Up at the Camp it took the trees on our east side,
It cleared the shoreline
of its boats and docks,
And blowing past,
It lifted branches,
Shingles,
Rocks.
It rearranged the landscape
every place it thundered through,
An angry rush of rain and wind,
Reshuffling and regurgitating underbrush.

AUTUMN—*ON HURRICANES*

The rotten trunks of trees felled on that afternoon
are still a part of Lockes' own wild topography.

But reckless,
Uncontrollable destruction,
Gave the grandest opportunity to bring the beauty back.
And so I let birch grow to build a better garden,
A grove of silver-white among the green.

We lost so many trees.
But what God tended,
Carefully amended,
Brought new hardy plants,
A gathering of white and silver ladies,
Elegantly decorating space and woods behind the Camp.

We Never Waste a Thing

All the colors that you see,
All the beauty
that is autumn's revelry,
Was born in 1938
in raging storm.
It took a hurricane
to sweep away the white pine forest,
Scrape it off the earth,
And fling its battered twigs and limbs,
Its sliced and slivered trunks,
Like shattered kindling,
Drifting woods in careless piles.
For miles and miles
the islands on the lake were rough debris,
Peculiar beds undone by wind.
They waited until ice was thick enough
to haul away the harvest
in their horse-drawn sleds.

The forest gardens,
First lay dormant.
Lost in shock,
And then a year or two or more
to build the soil up and start again.
And when the restless,

AUTUMN—WE NEVER WASTE A THING

Growing earth
gave back,
It gave bouquets of maple,
Birch,
And hemlock.

It gave up bushel after bushel,
Scraggly
bushes filled with raspberries.
It overflowed with raspberries,
Our pockets bulging,
Baskets swelling,
More than I could stuff into my mouth,
Delicious fruit.
We never waste a thing,
The fertile forest seemed to say.
My parents would agree.
They also never wasted anything,
And we were going to pick these berries,
Every single berry,
Every single morning,
Until not a single berry would be left to see.
It was an endless exercise in harvesting
that turned too soon to making juice,
And canning jam.
It seemed the quantities would never end.
I finally got so sick of picking,
Canning,
And preserving all this fruit,
I figured I would never eat the stuff.

MY MOTHER AND OTHER NEW ENGLANDERS

I had forgotten making do or do without
is carved into my DNA,
Is who I am.
And when it came
to savoring the fruits of my due diligence,
My strong distaste for autumn's grueling work
was quickly overcome by flavor,
Generous sweetness bursting in my mouth,
Enough to make me sing.

I never waste a thing.

Connections

She brought it back from home,
A hemlock in a paper cup,
To be a tree of memory,
Connecting her to other lives
and other places,
Hemlock that she knew,
That grew and thrived
between the water and the Camp.

It was a living thing
divining who she was,
Where she had been,
To where she now was firmly planted in,
Growing in a world of little girls
with polished shoes and pinafores,
Growing in a world
of math and physics floating in and out the doors,
Of cooking,
Always cooking for another meal,
Another Sunday dinner searching for some extra chairs.
Growing in a world of constant laundry,
Washing,
Folding,
Trudging up and down the stairs,
Tears and laughter,

MY MOTHER AND OTHER NEW ENGLANDERS

Relentless life that always pushed her forward
toward another day,
Another year,
Music filling all the sacred moments
as they hurried past.

But there it was,
The hemlock,
Standing,
Growing with her,
Spreading arms of grace
that brought back happiness and love—
The years of fishing with her brothers and her dad,
The years of riding in the boat to check the mail,
The years of sitting on the porch to talk,
The snapping peas and shucking corn,
The custard cups and chowder
often making up the meal,
The dandelion greens and cider—
All these brilliant flashes of her former life
were building bridges between water and the land,
Between her growing up in Concord
and her summers at the lake,
With everything that came to pass
beyond New England's granite house.
It settled her,
Quite comfortably
in fact,
That she who once was Yankee through and through
discovered sweet contentment further south.

Sanctifying Grace

He loved the gospel.
He just had trouble living it.
Day after day,
Person to person,
Father to child,
Husband to wife.
His life,
A magnificent stumble of starts and stops.
So hard to follow
the Savior's call,
Divine commands.

He heard them all,
But only as suggestions,
Blotted out by passing thoughts
that drifted in and out,
Distracting best intentions,
Shuffled,
Noticed,
Noted,
Shelved,
But seldom neatly filed
or carried out.

Yet God continued on,
He patiently pursued,
He loved this son with fortitude,
With holy courage
borne of bearing life's adversity,
Of wearing this man's pain and faltering
to break sin's sting,
And crush those things that kill the soul,
Undo those things that scatter thoughts,
That keep a man from tending,
Cultivating grace.

It was a constant,
Sacred task,
This taste for heaven
constantly intruding on a struggling heart.
It was a Sisyphean miracle
that truly overcame.

One trial at a time,
One passing misery reconstituted,
Redesigned,
Reclaimed for love,
For joy.
And day by day,
Step by step,
The shame peeled off,
The drifting died,
The suffering,
The guilt,

AUTUMN—SANCTIFYING GRACE

The strife,
Until one day,
The man,
At last
laid down the dying of himself
to gain a greater gospel life.

The Walk

The leaves fall down,
The world goes on.
Go about your work,
Do your work
with joy and laughter,
With gentleness and peace.

The leaves fall down,
They keep on falling.
And after the crawl,
The creeping sprawl
of entropy and sin,
I say it again,
Go about your work,
Do it all
with compassion and grace.

Live in truth,
Both near and far.
Stay on mission.
Love Christ first,
And then your neighbor.
Do not waver.

AUTUMN—THE WALK

Whatever you do,
Whenever you speak,
Whenever you buy,
Or sell,
Or plant and harvest
day after day,
Week after week,
Go about your work
wherever you are.

Last Fall

Nothing left but brown
and fading orange leaves,
Too few to dress a tree,
Just bits and pieces left
from better days,
When waving branches
danced and swayed to meet the wind,
And brimming buds
all burst with their own waking,
Turning into groves of lavish green,
Becoming red and orange flames,
And finally a mass of bristling twigs and sticks.
And so the dance went on
from year to year,
Until today,
When there was nothing left to see
but brown and fading orange leaves,
A whisp of tired fluttering,
Another leaf or two
to dance
before they flung themselves against the earth.
And all the weary stems,
Remembering,
Could feel the waltz within the winding down,
Could hear the laughing breezes

AUTUMN—LAST FALL

bending air to brush the tree,
Could sense the melody remaining,
Somewhere,
Packed away in all Creation,
Groaning until Consummation,
Waiting to be found.

Prayer for Consummation

O weary world,
Your weight is leaning hard on me
this morning.
In this hour,
Heavy clouds are dragging through the sky,
As if the soggy messiness of life
has tumbled in.
It finds already there,
The edginess within the air,
The rumbling,
Restless,
Flashing lights,
The fights within
our struggling selves.
And all the canopy above,
Can see us lugging all our miseries
from place to place,
And many in the firmament are watching,
Waiting,
Yearning
for the face of God,
When human pain,
When tears and rain
will be released,

AUTUMN—*PRAYER FOR CONSUMMATION*

and all the earth
will come again to perfect peace.

Winter

First Snow

White powdered sugar,
Shaken from the clouds
on worlds below,
A glistening icing,
Dusting trees and ground.
Blow it 'round!
Let lifting,
Flying crystals,
Dance across my face!
I smell the cold.
I feel the sharpness
in the air.
And everywhere is snow,
Is snow,
Is restless, flurrying snow!

Ghost Trees

The heavier snow is back,
The cold,
The wind that moans
around the house
and rocks the trees with shivering.
Whatever leaves are left
are shaken free
to dance and dash
their way to icy ground.
The green firs rustle quietly,
Stalwart matrons firmly planted,
Firmly placed to settle down.
But ghosting trees—
Their white bark shaping,
Spreading over growing arms
like branching skeletons—
They dip and sway.
Without their leaves
they might be camouflaged by snow.
But growing up
between the green,
They cannot hide,
And give the forest eerie contrasts.
Looking through the swirls of flakes,
Like long forgotten dreams,

WINTER—*GHOST TREES*

I see these shuddering ghosts
and memories of trees.

Winter Joy

Come, winter, come!
The snow is packed for sleighs.
We fourteen children
can't see any good
in walking down the hill to school.
Too long.
Too cold.
Too wet.
Besides, some dawdle over breakfast,
Making everyone arrive too late.
Drag out the double runner sled!
Time for the Cates to hit the road.
Some say they set their kitchen clocks
by when we Cates go whizzing by.
So clear a path,
And watch us fly!
We are a flash of screaming laughter,
Just a dash from hilltop
to the school yard down below.
The hardest part,
Of course,
Is going home.
By afternoon,
We are a line,
A caravan of trudging warriors,

Dragging,
Hauling back our mighty chariot,
A cloud of icy breath is wreathed above our heads.
It takes some serious work
to pull this heavy sled behind,
And halfway up,
Our sister, Nancy, thinks we could be warmer in our beds,
And someone whispers in the air,
I wish I was already there.
But oh, the bliss!
The rush each morning of the whistling wind across our face,
The sense that we are faster than the eagle flying overhead,
That for a breathless moment we can truly fly,
Can dash to glory,
Oh the wondrous, glorious ride!

Two Friends

Come winter,
John sets out the shanty on the ice.
Bob House, he calls it,
Dragging it by runners
out onto the frozen lake
to catch some fish.
And he and Charlie
settle into cribbage,
While the jigging line
entices cusk,
And perch,
And trout
to give the bait a try.
Cold work,
This waiting for the fish to bite.
The sun,
Still yawning,
Thinks it much too early yet
to melt the snow,
or interrupt such eager fishermen at work
with morning glare.
And even with the heater,
Conversation freezes in the air,
Good words mix vapor clouds with hearty laughs
as two friends pull in fish

WINTER—*TWO FRIENDS*

to fill their pails.
Good chowdah coming,
One says to the other.
His neighbor grunts and nods,
Good batch.
And so it goes,
The weekend catch.

In January

It looks just like a giant cave,
The sky above
all vaulted gray and dark,
The air asleep,
And I am deep in dreams.
So silently
the snow is falling.
Captured by the wind,
The flakes are blowing
back and forth across my face.
I feel their chill,
And wrap my scarf more tightly still.
Lumbering more slowly through the drifts,
It gives me pause to notice things—
The gathering of white,
Like mounded ice cream billowing on top of gates,
On cars,
On trees.
The freezing temperatures
have dripped enormous icicles,
Like grand stalactites,
Draped,
Cascading over second-story roofs.
Cold, so cold.
My front yard needs a blanket,

WINTER—IN JANUARY

So the snow
is bundling up a shivering world
with layer upon layer of its glistening stuff.
I've had enough.
Windows glow with fading light,
And I am thinking
time for something warm to drink.
There is an achiness about the place.
My breath,
So clearly visible,
Is clinging,
Hanging there.
Before I let this winter seep into my bones,
I trudge back through the growing deep.
Time to let this arctic dome
unpack its sharp and icy sleep.

XC Skiing

Chuff, chuff,
Slide and glide,
The skis lead me
across the trail.
Get the rhythm.
Find the pace.
It's not a race,
Just forward motion through the woods.
Chuff, chuff,
The only sounds my skiing makes
are buffered by the silent snow,
The snow heaped all along the roots,
And piled around the darkened trunks.
The snow that wraps and hugs
most everywhere I look
in deep luxurious blankets,
Mounding coverings of shimmering cold.
The snow,
So freshly groomed,
The route laid here before me,
Decorates the forest floor,
All gently ridged
like corduroy.
The snow that's flocked the hemlock and the pine,
And dresses lesser trees

WINTER—XC SKIING

in scarfs and mittens,
Bits of covering to keep away
the winter's icy edge.
A hedge or two have fluffy hats,
But that's the best she offers.
Wait 'til spring,
She seems to say,
If you want something warm.
We are asleep.
So quiet here,
Even a deer is listening in
as I deploy my skis and poles
across the path.
Chuff, chuff,
Uphill and down.
So many woods,
So many fields
in so much snow.
So little sound.

Skinning

Hitch the skins to wrap the skis
and hit the slopes,
I'm going up.
Good skins.
Good traction
on this rugged icy heap,
This crystal hill.
Hard climb.
Cold walk.
Trying to maximize the rhythm,
Trying to feel the beat.
The only heat
is aching muscles,
Tired legs,
And weary feet.
It's forcing me
to measure every stride and every breath.
How much farther must I go?
My poles dig deeper in,
And steady out a faltering step.
Only a hill,
Only some snow,
I think.
The path I'm making marks the route
to bring me back.

WINTER—*SKINNING*

So turn around,
I grumble,
Time to fly and feel the breeze.
Peel back the skins
and pack them up,
And let the winds and gravity
renew my fading energies.

The End of Talks

Lost for a season,
Cannot come back.
The road less traveled
becomes unraveled,
Her memories scattered,
Dancing on wind
like drying leaves.
Today we remember,
Tomorrow the words
are all too thin,
Too many cracks
to carry thoughts,
Or settle emotions,
Too veined with confusions
to comprehend what has been spoken
to let me in.
We both feel the coolness,
The briskness that shadows
meandering talks.
Pulling shawls ever tighter,
Our spirits are worn
as we huddle like underbrush,
Brittle and sharp.
Winter is coming.
Beware of storms.

The Girl Beneath

And the wheels slow down,
Roll slowly down.
The runner walks,
The walker leans upon a cane.
Sometimes she sits,
Sometimes she rests.

The carpool years of school
give way to grocery runs and Sunday church.
No more the endless lessons
crowding up the hours of her day.
Just weekly trips.
Necessities are lean and light,
And all too soon the driver rides.
Sometimes she sits,
Sometimes she stays
at home instead.
Too far.
Too long.
Lord, too much pain.

Where is the girl,
The one who played from
dawn to dusk?
Her all-expanding energies

MY MOTHER AND OTHER NEW ENGLANDERS

for high adventures,
Reveling in love,
In husband,
Children,
Laundry,
Cooking,
Scrubbing tubs.
Exalting in a well-lived life?

She still is there,
Tucked carefully inside,
Beneath the folds of weary skin and tired bones.
She did live well.
She lives well still.
And all the creases verify—
The laughing wrinkled eyes,
The stiff and aching hands
that often touched a baby's face.
The feet that trampled up and down,
And up and down again
to conquer stairs
and hallways in the name of Grace.

Her girls reflect her ardor
for a well-lived life—
Their years of laundry,
Ironed shirts,
And savory meals.
Their art.
Their music

WINTER—THE GIRL BENEATH

carries on the hidden girl
beneath this slower pace,
Beneath the pain that steals and wounds
the beauty
of her worn and weathered gaze.

So wheels slow down,
Roll slowly down.
Come take your rest.
For soon the girl
will rise again,
Will feel the morning sun,
And run the heights,
Will scramble up the rocks,
Content.
At last, content
to live, to be.
To know the joys of greater days.

My Mother's House

We aged together,
This house and I,
Two grand old ladies
wrestling time.
While living grays the edges,
Smudges faces,
Draws sweet lines,
Our style transformed
from fashion hip
to vintage.
We both are bent a bit,
And carry on our frames
the worn patina gained by years of love.

Love gives caresses,
Rubs too hard.
Love pouts.
Love slams.
It reprimands.
It seeks forgiveness,
Offers more.
It opens windows,
Closes doors.
It shelters from the heat and cold.
It creaks.

WINTER—MY MOTHER'S HOUSE

It moans.
It tests the range of human
rage and suffering by light,
And in the night
it stills the storms.
Love never ends.
But human warranties and homes
have "use by" dates.
We both have reached
our mending days—
Adjustments here,
Or fixes there—
Necessities with all the wear and tear
brought on by life.

In many ways,
While sharing almost sixty years of space,
I am the house,
I am the home.
And this constructed edifice
that carries me,
It, too, reflects my heart and hopes.
And so we move together,
Harder now to separate the one
who is the tenant,
From the other.
So many years,
So many memories entwined.

MY MOTHER AND OTHER NEW ENGLANDERS

A house.
A woman.
Two old ladies stand.
Both lives in vibrant history combined.

Pilgrim Faith

He is loving me through
the agonies of life,
When I hope for death,
For an end to pain,
Where I would disdain to press on
one more day.
How I long for home,
And He makes me stay.
So I wrestle on.
The box shrinks down,
The rooms grow small,
More *can't* than *can*,
With each and every painful step.

But His Word is true.
His care is covering me everywhere.
He lifts my heart.
He feeds my mind,
And I find whispers of His blessings,
All His gentleness descending
on my laboring soul.
Old woman,
Tired woman,
I have engraved your name
on the palms of my hands.

MY MOTHER AND OTHER NEW ENGLANDERS

My arms are wide,
Wide enough
to carry your load and set you free.
So I say to myself,
Let this house stand
as long as He
would have me run this course.
Just one more day,
And then another,
One more hour
until He comes to make me whole.

In Step

Every day I climb a mountain.
Every day I hike a mile.
Simple efforts constantly are changing,
Rearranging,
Metamorphosing through endless tasks.
It is a challenge every day to make me last.

And so I ask for gifts of grace to make it through.
I'm asking You,
Lord,
Give me strength to carry on.
The days are long.
The nights of rest are short.
For every step I gain,
I lose too many more to count.
I want to be Your good and faithful servant
all my days,
Not just the ones that mark an easier path,
But all the days that test my perseverance and my faith,
The ones that leave me panting
as I run the race.
The ones I wonder how I'll make it through the gate.
Those are the days I revel in Your glorious presence,
Always lifting,
Always making me aware I never am alone.

MY MOTHER AND OTHER NEW ENGLANDERS

The days Your arms
hold me the most securely I have ever known,
Those are the days my heart,
My mind,
My steps are right in step with You.
It is a challenge every single day to make me last.
And so I ask You, dearest friend,
For gifts of grace to make it through.

More

Should I hold tightly
to the one who
held so tightly on to me?

No.
Let her go.

She is much better held
in Jesus' arms
than mine.
And in His love,
His word-defining,
Arms-held-wide forgiveness,
Sweet compassion
mixed with mercy,
He is more than she or I have ever known.

It's hard to say goodbye.

But you will see her face again
in better worlds,
In better circumstances,
More extraordinary,
More magnificent,
More glorious

than any mind or heart could dare imagine.
All without the pain and sorrow
burying this world.

So let her go.
Let Grace and Glory
make her more than she has ever been.
There is an end to sin,
And she is now eclipsed
by never-ending grand eternity.
Let His own story
be her righteousness and peace.
Let Life begin!

Until He Comes

Winter here
is full of blue and brown,
Where steel sky hovers over barren ground,
With endless fields of prickly brooms
turned upside down.

This forest full of bristle brushes,
Seems to bend and lean toward growing clouds,
So cold,
Their woody arms reach out to hold each other fast.
Air so still,
A whisper sounds too loud,
A creaking wind a bit too brash.
The chilled still wait for all the promised hope of rain and snow.
No birds to break the silence here below.

For once in ancient days
a baptism of washing
scrubbed out all the vanities of man from earth.
And while we wait for fire and for grace,
He covers up a multitude of sins
by dressing life's dark restlessness in cold and snow.

But someday,
When the sun returns among the blue

to warm the day,
And bring His light,
The rustling brown will laugh for all the chattering,
The choirs of Creation trumpeting
the end of death at last.
And only He will know
when birds are meant to stay.
For only then will winters cease,
And spring will never pass away.

Now, Not Yet

She goes to sleep each night
expecting to wake up into eternity.
Lord, give her grace
to face today,
The aches and pains,
The struggling places she would rather leave,
This world and all its agony.
Lord, give her hope
that You are here,
Already rescuing this tired soul,
And soon will usher her into her perfect rest.
Lord, give her strength
to see Your mighty hand,
To know
that she will make it through each waking hour.
And as she sees again her many sorrows
still in place,
And grieves the darkness in the night,
Lord, be her fortress while she waits.

Grace

Learning how to lean on Him
amid the sadness of this world,
The pain,
The loss,
The limitations—
All these drag me down,
They bruise the muscles of my soul
to hold such weight.
My heart is heavy for the one You love,
How low must this one go?
The road of suffering goes farther down,
Still farther down.
Yet somewhere in the dark,
I know that she and I are not alone.
My yoke is easy,
You have said,
My burden light.
Lord,
Take this ponderous sorrow,
Take the load.
Lord,
Carry us,
We who struggle every step,
We who pray
and sometimes wonder if we're heard,

WINTER—GRACE

And worry that our daily lives
are just another test.
Come to me,
You say,
And you who labor
and are heavy laden,
I will give you rest.

Waiting

Winter woods lay bare their other natures.
What was hidden in the summer and the fall
is suddenly revealed—
The random piles of leaves
like absent-minded lumps of laundry,
Remnants of the trees undressing,
Changing ladies caught
between
their spring and summer clothes
with nothing left to wear.
Yet all their damp,
Discarded layers
are forgotten,
As the snows soon come
to wrap these shivering underdressers
into robes of dreams,
Where those preoccupied by sleep
now wait for longer days and warmer air.
The undulating hills and vales,
Shaping,
Molding forest floor,
Create a carpet rich in scattered bits of memories
that once were vibrant life,
And now are only recollections and decay.

WINTER—WAITING

The spring will come.
Lulled for now by dormancy,
The winter weathers on,
A thought,
A promise slumbering within the tomb,
A melody of grace awaiting harmony and consummation,
Gathering the Truth from ancient store,
Until all waiting ends,
Until there are no secrets anymore.

A Time to Heal

He has put eternity
into the old man's heart,
And heaven's grace will not depart
until the man is safely home.
To all of us who travel here
alongside him,
On this desperate road,
This highway filled with stumbling,
His final moments overwhelmed
by our anxieties and fears,
(He who meets his final labor,
Robbed of energies,
And taking ours)
I tell you all,
Be now at peace.

He will endure.
Not here.
Now now,
But for forever,
Far beyond our sight.
For He who made this man,
Has claimed him,
Beautiful,
Beloved.

WINTER—A TIME TO HEAL

And all our reckoning,
Our wrestling here
is fast becoming this man's restoration,
He, no longer meant for us,
But for a world that has no night.

Their Last Battle

Now they are gone,
Good fellows
on the road into the Promised Land.
Their road—
It has been difficult,
Some days and nights
a dreadful thing.
But that's the wilderness,
They'd say,
And we have braved its torrents
and its searing winds,
And who can stray
beyond the bounds
that God allows,
But bravely walk the path,
Be faithful,
Ever faithful to the last.
We,
Those left behind,
We stand in quiet awe.
Though often faltering,
These trembling souls
were constantly enduring,
Leaning on their Father's arms.
These earnest pilgrims

WINTER—*THEIR LAST BATTLE*

took their loss in hand.
They did not cower on the journey home.
They walked with earnestness,
They lived by faith.
Their steadiness to stay the course,
Became their stand.

Mount Hope Cemetery, Loudon

I walked across another cemetery,
Looking for a family name
among the gravestones planted in a field of leaves.
So many there,
So many lean
as if the weight of years
is ever bowing down the very markers
meant to celebrate the tired bodies resting underneath.
Here lies,
They say, or,
In Memory of,
As words relate a life
from date to date.
Some lives too young,
And older members trying to explain
what cut their lives so short.
Centuries of weather
streak the stones with darker grays,
And eat at funerary art displays.
Skulls with wings,
And words all fading into crevices,
Their message blending into light and shadows,
Poignant commentary on our own mortality.

WINTER—MOUNT HOPE CEMETERY, LOUDON

It is a gathering of neighbors
even after death.

Stone near stone near stone,
A congregation bound up to their God
and to each other,
Lives preparing for eternity.
Each in their own space,
But not alone.

I find the names.

I, too, am bound up to eternity.
And when I find my family,
I marvel just how much I feel at home.
I am connected
to the relatives that came before.
They are resting, waiting.
Only dates and names for now.

I am wandering among the stones,
I, too, waiting for the Day
when all my aunts, and uncles,
Cousins, grand and great grands meet me in the air,
And we recount the mysteries of grace
that presently are silent underground.

He Is My Rock

When the years of shadows come,
Remember,
God has never left.
He is not waiting in the wings for summoning,
Not buried deep within
the scattered debris of our restless pain
where wanderings of mind and heart
lean ever downward,
Further from sweet hope and closer to the grave.
Such anguish clutters up our faith,
Diminishing our confidence.
We say we cannot cope.
He sees.
He knows.
We never walk the shadows by ourselves,
We never stand alone.
We may be wavering as infants,
One foot forward,
Then another,
Nervous fingers reaching everywhere,
Precariously balanced,
Caught between His surety of grace
and our own helpless fear.
He still is near.
He does not leave.

WINTER—*HE IS MY ROCK*

Even a single breath
is gently gifted
to the one who fights for air.

Hope

I sometimes think
that winter never ends—
The rolling fog
that hugs the snow,
The endless gray,
The freezing rain—
And then one day
I see a robin
perched atop the fence,
Inviting sun to come again,
Reminding vacant woods
to flourish,
Full of sap and green.
And I remember
that until He comes,
Until His work is done,
Seasons follow seasons,
Awakening will follow sleep,
And spring will come.

Remembering

Remembering

So many snapshots of my past
are tugging at my heart.
Here is my chance
to redefine my energies,
And recognize the ever-changing,
Shifting-sand priorities that mark my life.
Slow down,
I say.
Be grateful for another day,
Another year.
Be thankful for my family,
The opportunity to revel in another birth,
Another fledgling infant
suddenly
(My, how time flies!)
a graduate,
And I see generations racing by.

I am aware.

I touch the memories of those
already gone.
I see their faces,
Hear their voices in my head,
A permanent display of pictures,

MY MOTHER AND OTHER NEW ENGLANDERS

Some with sound,
The others just a moment caught
within a sigh,
A scene that takes me
one more time
into a dream,
That takes me walking through the woods,
Or capturing the sound of boats,
The slap of waves against the rocks.

Time keeps ticking,
Forging on ahead.
I cannot stop its forward motion.
I am living in its moving clock.
But I can file away the sounds,
The passing moments,
Heady things,
Like sweet aromas,
Pulling me back into places I have been.
Perhaps today I shall camp there a bit
and sit,
And wonder at it all.

The Old Stone House

Hiram built a house of stone.
He owned the rolling landscape
up and over various hills,
And down a way into the village,
Not too far from Loudon Town,
His home a favored place to stay.
Oak Hill was a perfect spread for horses and a barn.
It had a sheep pen with its own stone wall,
A cider mill around the back,
And room enough to house the hired help who ran the farm.

Even when his son
became the owner,
Hospitality spilled over.
One friend remembers
heading out to visit at the farm.
They'd sit a spell and talk.
Before too long,
An offering of food was made.
Perhaps some tea or something sweet,
A neighbor always offers something good to eat.

Charles, the son,
Thought that his mother and his father should stay on,
And so they did.

MY MOTHER AND OTHER NEW ENGLANDERS

And then Charles took his daughter Nancy in,
When her own John had died,
And welcomed in her sons.
What's three more in this spacious home?
Big enough to raise a host of children.
Hiram and his wife had three,
Two boys,
One girl.
And then his son and wife
had fourteen more,
One room for girls,
Another room for boys.

As time went by,
The grand piazza slouched.
Still soldiering on,
The various sheds and outer buildings
leaned a little more,
And tottered closer to the house.
It had been carrying and cradling one generation with another,
So many people blessed by generosity and grace,
Until one day,
Its fading dignity and aging wood collapsed.

The monument,
It seems,
Was not the pile of rubble in the cellar,
But the way the building stood
(Within its time)
between its occupants

REMEMBERING—*THE OLD STONE HOUSE*

and all the storms that hurry strife.
And by the way the people sheltered by its stone and mortar,
Lived and labored with each other,
Passing down,
One to another,
All the fragrances that sweeten life.

Hiram 1807–1892

Grandpa said
that Hiram was a sport,
The sort that came from money.
The sort that gathered usefulness in what he had,
And did not waste,
But generously bestowed in both
his public and his private life.
Cash enough to own a track in Loudon
where he raced his horses,
Cash enough to buy a decent piece of property,
And build a house
with barns and sheds,
A cider mill,
A smithy,
And with land enough for half a hogshead,
Sheep pen,
And a sloping cow yard for the stock.

And from the hilltop,
Overlooking Loudon Village,
He surveyed his holdings,
Wondering,
Amazed what goodness God had wrought,
And thanked Him for the giving to his grateful heart
a Mary

to bring children to his life.
And when she died,
An Abigail
to walk him through the years remaining.
Certain in a joy that follows sorrow,
Constant in a faith sustaining
those that knew this gracious soul.

And with this bounty,
He had time enough to be a consult for the local doctor,
Time enough to serve the town of Loudon,
Making sure community and congregation
met together on the field of conviviality and fellowship
in times of war.
And in the rainy weather,
When the harvesting was put on hold,
He made the time enough for fun,
And took his hearty men up north
to trek as far as Canada,
In search of fresh, delicious trout.

God gave him time enough
to do the jobs at hand.
He took the time, and spent it well,
Spent every cent,
Left nothing to his heirs in cash,
But plenty in wise counsel,
Much in independent thinking,
Careful tilling,
Good management of land.

MY MOTHER AND OTHER NEW ENGLANDERS

He was a caring friend,
A generous neighbor.
Those who knew him
said he worked as hard,
He played as hard,
He lived as hard as any man.

Nancy 1868–1961

She married Frank
at twenty-one,
Too young to know yet
just how circumstances
change the very air you breathe.

Until the well went bad.

The boys survived.
But Frank
and baby Harriet
did not.
A husband barely thirty,
And the baby—
Lost.
One day,
One helpless day.

Hard life,
She said,
Hard life,
And felt the weight of dying
bury her,
And pour its miseries upon her head.

MY MOTHER AND OTHER NEW ENGLANDERS

For seven years
she was a single mom.
Make do,
She said,
I have already done without.
Make do,
By tatting package string
for oven mitts and table pads.
Make do,
By cleaning all the clocks yourself.
Make do,
By making your own soap.
Make do,
By cobbling your shoe repairs.
Whatever else you have
that must be done
or done about,
Make do,
Or do without.

One boy settled with the Maynards.
One boy settled with the Cates.
She needed work.
The mortuary needed staff.
Anything to bring in money
and to keep her sane.
Her heart still leaning
toward the cemetery,
Thought preparing bodies

REMEMBERING—NANCY 1868–1961

for their burial
might ease the pain.

Somewhere on the way,
Nancy rediscovered life,
And chose to care for living people,
Giving grace to tired bodies,
Weary hearts and minds.
She needed more.

Emma needed someone
who would have compassion,
Someone who could love the person,
And respect the fragile body that they wore.
So Nancy labored day by day to care for Emma,
Washing,
Dressing,
Listening,
Nursing aging Emma down the road
that separates a shriveling frame
from all its earthly sorrows,
All its pain,
'Til Life and Emma's death eclipsed it all.
Life is hard,
Nancy said.
Life is hard.
And she and Emma
shared those words
together,

MY MOTHER AND OTHER NEW ENGLANDERS

On the road
that took this Emma home to God.

And then there are two people left—
A grieving man.
A woman caring for his wife.
Both of them in emptiness.
Each of them has known alone.
They carry it from room to room.
It fills the spaces in between them,
Making walls of solitude.
He is worrying,
Still concerned that it might show.
She is hoping
no one near would ever know.
The one saw in the other
someone who could take what life could throw,
Could rise above it all and grow
in spite of difficulties,
Searing circumstances,
And strife.
It seemed so right
to bring such fortitude together
in one house.
And so they did,
For thirty years.
The years when Nettie married John,
When Walter and his Nina made a life,
When there were babies in the house again.

REMEMBERING—NANCY 1868–1961

It went too fast.
It always does.
But they made happiness
of what they had,
As best they could.
Hard times,
She said,
Hard times,
But also, good.

Charles died in '32,
The Great Depression
draining all the promises of greater days,
The possibilities of things.
It couldn't touch the memories,
It couldn't take away
what she had been with him.

It couldn't take away
the early breakfast each and every morning with her John,
Or joining with his family
who lived above the stairs.
She was alone,
Yet not alone,
Surrounded by the ones she loved.

The day she died,
She washed the windows,
All the tall Victorian windows,
Bringing light into her life.

MY MOTHER AND OTHER NEW ENGLANDERS

She wouldn't go
until her work was done,
Until the time had come
to put her striving down,
And gain a better home instead.
She went to bed,
And in the lying down
she laid aside the sorrows,
All the troubles,
All the trials of her world.
She let them go.
Their sting removed,
Their power dispossessed,
She left,
And woke into eternal rest.

Hard life,
She said to Sylvia,
Hard life.
And so it was.
But also filled with promises of grace,
Where making do,
Or do without,
Had underpinned a legacy,
And given shape and energies
to her endurance,
In its ponderous wake.

John 1893–1988

God came close to him.
He didn't notice right away
that God was there.
He was too busy,
Being,
Trying to embrace whatever came his way.
But in his life,
The tender hand
of One who loved him as a son already,
Shared His blessings,
One by one.
There were so many that He shared—
A mother's faithful, giving love.
A father
all too soon removed by death,
Yet somehow left in memories.
A second dad
to help him navigate his hopes and dreams.
A grand extended family
close at hand,
To teach him humor,
And hard work,
Both buried deep within
a thousand points of character that shaped his soul.
That sense of continuity,

MY MOTHER AND OTHER NEW ENGLANDERS

That life had given him a certain role,
That he was part
of something greater than even he could hold.
A wife who loved him patiently,
And with a certain gentle grace.
Two strong sons
to carry on his reputation and his name,
They both resembling his style and sense of place.
A daughter,
More like him than all the rest,
So many ways the same.
Good, steady work
to exercise his hands
and stretch his mind.
Grandchildren,
Then great grands.
He was a man most blessed.
And he assumed
it was because he'd lived an honest life.
And in so many ways
he had.
So, God came closer still.
And suddenly
this man discovered what that greater thing had been,
And why he needed Him.
That there was more to truth
than in a fellow's name.
That there was more to faithfulness than steady work,
More beauty to be found
than everything and everyone he loved.

REMEMBERING—JOHN 1893–1988

That to be cherished
by the God who had been guiding,
Shaping,
Changing,
Rearranging every part of this man's very core—
From birth to final breath,
From passing thought
to blood and bone—
Was more important,
More essential,
More magnificent
than anything that he had ever dreamed about or known.

By Faith: Nettie 1895-1986

It must be difficult
to live in one world,
When it is so thoroughly becoming someplace else.
There were the usual disasters—
Fire in the factory,
Explosion of a coal mine,
Tornado devastation.
Terrible,
But sadly, not unusual in any given year.
But there was also raw rebellion in the air.
The Bolsheviks inciting violence
among a weary people far away,
Germany out flexing military muscles,
Interfering with their neighbors,
Driving nation after nation into war.
And underneath,
The social fabric of American society was fraying,
So many of the underlying rules,
That's the way we've always done it,
Giving way to silent protests
by the suffragettes,
Pleading for a woman's right to vote,
Race-related barbarism,
And then the Spanish Flu unloaded death
in all its eager breathlessness,

REMEMBERING—BY FAITH: NETTIE 1895–1986

As if a greater sense of gruesome winnowing,
A deadly harvesting
was now at play,
With every neighborhood found wanting,
Every nation shaken through the sieve.
In such a world,
How does a person live?
Nettie chose to live by faith.
She went to Plymouth Normal School,
And trained to be a teacher.
First in Whitefield,
Then in Roland Park.
She didn't stay the year
because she caught the influenza and pneumonia,
And it forced her home.
But she survived,
And went on teaching for a few more years,
(Before she married John)
A one-room schoolhouse teacher
of the lower grades,
The grades of grammar,
Penmanship,
Arithmetic and history,
The years of prioritizing what was best and right,
The days of putting what she could not change
aside,
For whom she knew would see her through.
And all around,
The world went on.
It did not stay the same as it had been.

It never does.
The comfort she derived
was not in ordinary lives,
Nor ordinary circumstance,
But in the One who rescued her,
From year to year,
From day to day,
That planted her a teacher for a season,
Planted her into her life with John,
Her life with two boys and a girl,
Her life that one day intersected with my own.
And I am better off for having known this woman
and her quietness,
Her strong devotion to the living God,
Her understanding of her tender place within the universe,
When all around,
The world stayed constantly in furious upheaval.

Never wasting moments on despair,
So hard to bend,
But always pressing forward in the fight,
Doing the next thing that came along,
She made the most of what was offered her in grace,
She kept the faith.

Waiting in the Shadows: Sylvia 1929–

She's in the shadows,
Farther from the camera,
Not in step
or time with all the others,
Walking her own way,
At her own pace,
Less space required than the wiggly children,
Adults all trying to present
a perfect pose and face,
Expressions practiced
over many interviews with mirrored glass.

She wishes her own minute hand would move as fast.

She's in the shadows now,
But she spent long years in the light,
She was the sun,
And all five whirling, twirling planets
(In their princess dresses)
danced in orbits synchronized
around her,
Marching to her drum throughout the day.

She was the dinner on the table,
Piano teacher,

MY MOTHER AND OTHER NEW ENGLANDERS

Bible study leader,
On the board of Christian school,
Dedicated driver for her daughters' music lessons,
An accompanist at church,
A tailor,
Teacher,
Gardener,
Hovering, demanding mother—
Practice! Practice!
Have you made your bed?
Brushed your teeth?
You're sitting. Fold—
Loving and supporting wife,
A comforter in everybody's life.

Her clock is winding down,
Stretching out in moments now
instead of days and years.
One step,
And then another.
Step. Stop. Step.

She's in the shadows,
Counting out the days
until she moves her orbit into His,
His Son,
His brightness greater than hers ever was.
She does not mind the fading,
Waiting is the hardest part.
Resting difficult when Christ and heaven is her gain.

REMEMBERING—*WAITING IN THE SHADOWS: SYLVIA 1929–*

Her slow and steady forward motion
leans into a sturdy cane.

Nelson 1938–

From early years
he saw the stars,
And wondered
at their bright immensity
so far from earth.
The science
found him questioning
at what he saw.
The fact of their creation
gave him awe
in his Creator.
He was taught the beauty
in the math,
The calculations necessary
underlying all the particles in space.
He thought of possibilities,
The grandeur
of a man exploring,
Spending all his life unpacking
all the intricacies,
All the vast exquisite details
of the universe displayed before his face.
What kind of universe
did this inventive God create?
What were the elements

REMEMBERING—NELSON 1938–

that painted an aurora borealis
in its shimmering
and mesmerizing swaths
across the sky?
What did it take
to make the heavens as they are,
The planets
as they fly and dance
around the sun,
The shadows of the moon
that stroke the world
and pull the tide?

Not long enough a life
to answer every question asked,
Or conquer every mystery.
But surely time enough
to open up a multitude
of curious conundrums,
To give this man a chance
to carefully unwrap
(At least a little bit)
what caused such splendors in the light,
And gain a clearer understanding
of the properties and glories
that this keen observer
witnessed every night.

The more he knew,
The more it turned

his heart to God,
To worshipping the One
who crafted what he loved.
Too young to truly contemplate
the measure of it all,
He had not watched the skies
a thousand years,
Or wrested all the meaning
from the months he had.
Too old to carry on the work
beyond the days that God allowed.
But just enough to shout,
How great you are, My God!
To raise his voice
in eulogies of praise.
To find that all he ever knew or ever would
was infinitesimally smaller
than the One to whom he bowed.

Gathered In

We've done rare things,
She writes,
A sacred harmony connecting truth and promises
to everyday belief,
A tedious,
Generous ordinary,
Has captured all the wisps
and breaths of hope,
And woven them
into my each and every ordinary day.

So come you thankful people,
Come and sing!
The music was already there, you see,
The actions cast,
The words put down.
The Father's will
explored the paper long before the writings made,
And wrote with glorious fingers
straight across the walls,
And up the stairs,
And into all the nooks and crannies waiting to be found.

His glory tempered rash ideas,
It rescued raveling thoughts,

And wove together such a life,
That looking back,
Amidst the sorrows and the cares,
She saw such richness—
Not in stuff,
She never had what other people
thought might be enough—
But in the people,
In her day-to-day existence
trudging up and down,
Up and down,
Cooking,
Cleaning,
Keeping up with all the goodness
wrapped around her,
Knowing He was present everywhere.

Even if the winter storms begin,
He will not fail,
She says,
And I will sing the song of Harvest,
I will sing,
And praise Him still.
I am content,
For soon I will be gathered in.

Genealogy of Key Ancestors

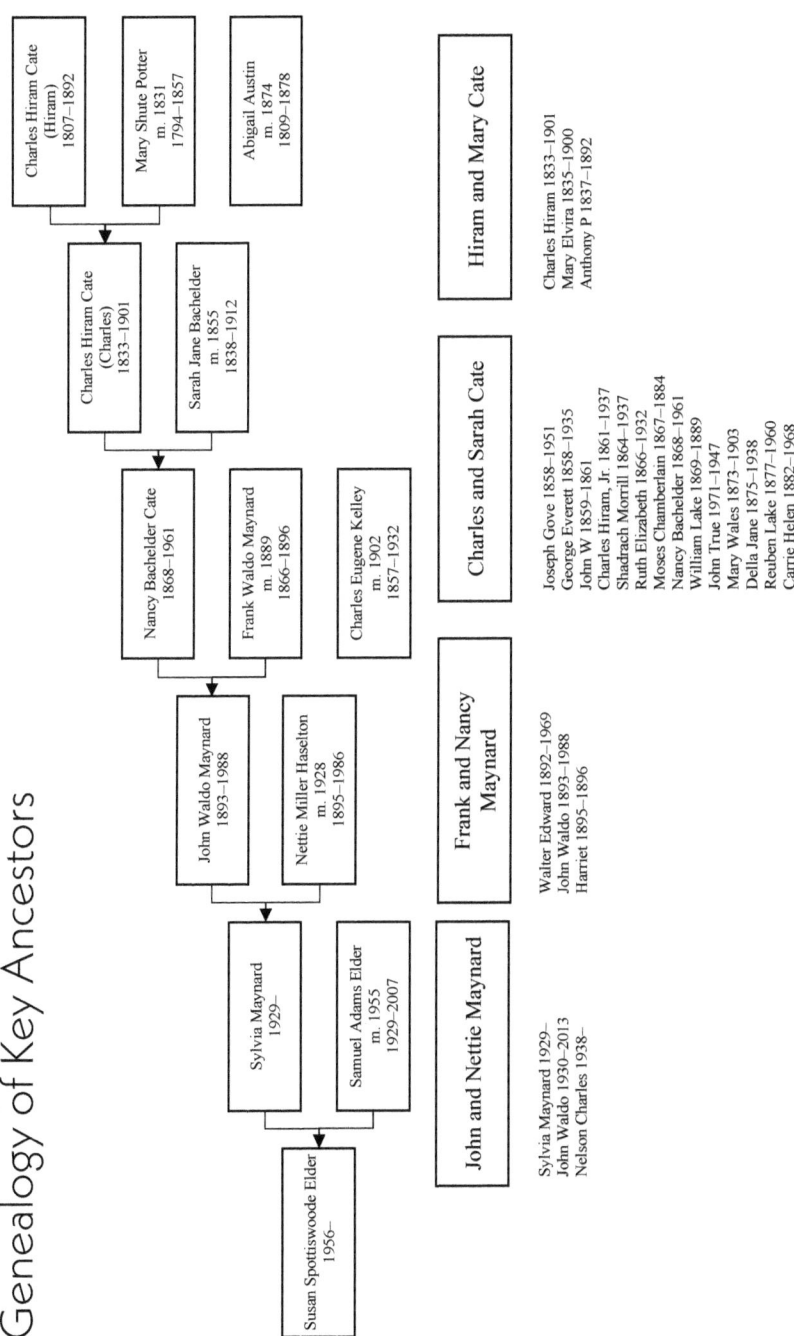

193

www.ingramcontent.com/pod-product-compliance
Lightning Source LLC
Chambersburg PA
CBHW051924160426
43198CB00012B/2029